Sex education

Sex
Education

Other books in the At Issue series:

Affirmative Action
Are Efforts to Reduce Terrorism Successful?
Are the World's Coral Reefs Threatened?
Club Drugs
Do Animals Have Rights?
Does the World Hate the United States?
Do Infectious Diseases Pose a Serious Threat?
Do Nuclear Weapons Pose a Serious Threat?
The Ethics of Capital Punishment
The Ethics of Euthanasia
The Ethics of Genetic Engineering
The Ethics of Human Cloning
Fast Food
Food Safety
Gay and Lesbian Families
Gay Marriage
Gene Therapy
How Can School Violence Be Prevented?
How Should America's Wilderness Be Managed?
How Should the United States Withdraw from Iraq?
Internet Piracy
Is Air Pollution a Serious Threat to Health?
Is America Helping Afghanistan?
Is Gun Ownership a Right?
Is North Korea a Global Threat?
Is Racism a Serious Problem?
The Israeli-Palestinian Conflict
Media Bias
The Peace Movement
Reproductive Technology
Should Juveniles Be Tried as Adults?
Teen Suicide
Treating the Mentally Ill
UFOs
What Energy Sources Should Be Pursued?
What Motivates Suicide Bombers?
Women in the Military

Sex
Education

Kristen Bailey, *Book Editor*

Bruce Glassman, *Vice President*
Bonnie Szumski, *Publisher*
Helen Cothran, *Managing Editor*

GREENHAVEN PRESS
An imprint of Thomson Gale, a part of The Thomson Corporation

THOMSON

---*---

GALE

Detroit • New York • San Francisco • San Diego • New Haven, Conn.
Waterville, Maine • London • Munich

For more information, contact
Greenhaven Press
27500 Drake Rd.
Farmington Hills, MI 48331-3535
Or you can visit our Internet site at http://www.gale.com

LIBRARY OF CONGRESS CATALOGING-IN-PUBLICATION DATA
Sex education / Kristen Bailey, book editor.
p. cm. — (At issue)
Includes bibliographical references and index.
ISBN 0-7377-2418-8 (lib. : alk. paper) — ISBN 0-7377-2419-6 (pbk. : alk. paper)
1. Sex instruction—United States. I. Bailey, Kristen. II. At issue (San Diego, Calif.)
HQ57.5.A3S47 2005
613.9'071—dc22   2004049293

Printed in the United States of America

Contents

Page

Introduction   6

1. The Sex Education Debate: An Overview   10
   Molly Masland

2. Sex Education Has Failed   15
   Center for AIDS Prevention Studies

3. Sex Education Has Succeeded   20
   William R. Finger

4. Abstinence Education Is the Most Effective Way to Protect Teen Health   29
   Robert E. Rector

5. Most Parents Advocate Abstinence Education for Their Children   41
   The Abstinence Clearinghouse

6. Advocates of Abstinence Education Are Hypocrites   45
   Sarah Goff

7. Comprehensive Sex Education Is the Most Effective Way to Protect Teen Health   49
   John P. Elia

8. Comprehensive Sex Education Does Not Work   59
   Kerby Anderson

9. The Politics of Sex Education Debates   67
   Janice M. Irvine

10. Teen Sexual Risk Taking Is Reduced by Attending School   78
    Douglas Kirby

11. The Mass Media Educate Youth About Sex   90
    Jane D. Brown and Sarah N. Keller

12. Sex Education Should Address the Needs of Gay Teens   95
    Carol Lee

Organizations to Contact   101

Bibliography   104

Index   107

Introduction

According to a survey by the Heritage Foundation, only 7 percent of parents are happy with the sex education curricula that are offered in America's schools. It can be difficult to find a sexuality education program that meets the needs of all children. Abstinence curricula, which teach that sex should be delayed until marriage, ignore the needs of teens who are already sexually active and need to be educated on birth control and sexually transmitted diseases. Comprehensive curricula, which acknowledge that many teens will become sexually active, teach about contraception as well as sexually transmitted diseases, including HIV and AIDS. Many parents fear that comprehensive programs may encourage sexual activity among teens by teaching them how to have safe sex and minimizing the abstinence message.

Many experts contend that dissatisfaction with school sex education programs should be addressed by encouraging parents to begin sex education at home. As with math, reading, and other areas of study, it is impossible for a school-based education program that takes place in a large group setting to meet the unique needs of each and every student. Parents know their own children better than anyone else and can therefore tailor sex education lessons to their individual child's needs. Most experts who recommend that sex education be taught at home recognize that parents may need guidance. According to SIECUS, the Sexuality Information and Education Council of the United States,

> Parents are—and ought to be—their children's primary sexuality educators, but may need help and encouragement to fulfill this important role. Religious leaders, youth and community group leaders, and health and education professionals can complement and augment the sexuality education that takes place at home.

If parents begin to educate their children about sex at home, school programs can become more of a supplement to that education, perhaps increasing parental satisfaction with such programs. Unfortunately, many Americans feel uncomfortable discussing sexuality with their children. Many parents today were raised during a time when sex was not something that was discussed openly, if at all. The Planned Parenthood organization, as part of its Family Communication Series of literature, offers this advice to hesitant parents: "Don't cover up your feelings or avoid the issue. That will make matters worse. Start a conversation, keep it going, and be open from the beginning. Just remember—information about sexuality is as important as food, shelter, and loving care."

Other advice offered by organizations concerned about teens and sex is that parents need not feel that they have to cover all the issues in one sitting. These experts claim that just being open to frank conversations about sex will help parents keep their children safe. According to Avert, the international HIV and AIDS charity,

> Viewing sex education as an on-going conversation about values, attitudes and issues as well as providing facts can be helpful. The best basis to proceed on is a sound relationship in which a young person feels able to ask a question or raise an issue if they feel they need to. It has been shown that in countries like The Netherlands, where many families regard it as an important responsibility to talk openly with children about sex and sexuality, this contributes to greater cultural openness about sex and sexuality and improved sexual health among young people.

However, simply talking openly about sex with children is not enough. Parents must also make their own stance about teenage sexual activity clear. A study by Stephen Small from the University of Wisconsin–Madison and Tom Luster at Michigan State University, published in the *Journal of Marriage and the Family*, found that parental involvement and communication of parents' values were significant factors in preventing and delaying teen sexual activity. They argue, "Permissive parental values regarding adolescent sexual behavior emerged as a strong risk factor for both males and females. Not surprisingly, adolescents who perceived their parents as accepting of premarital adolescent sexual activity were more likely to be sexually experienced."

The Small and Luster study raises the question of whether

parental discussions about sex can actually lead to more sexual activity. This is a fear that many parents of teenagers face. The concern is that by talking to children about sex parents are actually giving them permission to be sexually active, even promiscuous. For example, a mother who purchases condoms for her teenage son to help him protect himself from disease may worry that he might see her action as tacit permission to have sex. This fear is one that parents can set aside, according to the organization Advocates for Youth. Parents can use their "sex talks" to make their morals known and prevent any second-guessing on the part of their teens. The organization explains:

> Parents need to provide moral guidelines. . . . Given the fact that many adolescents engage in sex without their parents' consent, adults can try to ensure that these sexual encounters are not disastrous. Standards of behavior are good for adolescents, as well as for adults. Adolescents want and need sensible guidelines from their parents.

Parents may be reticent to discuss sex with their children, but getting past their discomfort can protect their children's health, and could even save their lives. Statistics from the Centers for Disease Control and Prevention show that young people between the ages of fifteen and twenty-four account for approximately half of all new HIV infections in the world, and represent almost a third of the total global population living with HIV and AIDS. Another reason why sex education should begin, and continue to take place at home is that children need to hear this vital information more than once. Many sex education programs, even those in high schools, take place for only a week or two before a regular health or physical education program is reinstated in its place. But children need to hear information about sex and disease over and over. According to the National Parent Teacher Association:

> Talk again and again. Don't think that a one-time discussion is all that is necessary. You want to have discussions about HIV/AIDS with your children early and often. Having these conversations with your children at different ages provides them with more in-depth information on the subject as they grow in their understanding of concepts such as disease, death, and sex.

In the book *How to Talk to Your Child About Sex: It's Best to Start Early, but It's Never Too Late,* authors Linda and Richard Eyre advise answering questions about sex when a child is as young as three, and having a "big talk" with children once they reach the age of eight. They claim beginning sex education at home can work wonders toward helping children have healthy future relationships:

> The evidence is overwhelming that any parent who puts his or her mind to it, and who has the confidence of the right approach and the right tools, can teach a child to view sex positively and responsibly; that a parent can protect his or her child from the devastating physical and emotional dangers of experimental, casual, or promiscuous sexual activity and enhance the child's chance for a stable, happy, committed marriage and family.

According to a 2004 survey by the Alan Guttmacher Institute, rates of pregnancy, birth, and abortion among U.S. teenagers have continued to fall steadily, and, since peaking in 1990, have continued to decline. Sex experts attribute this decline to sex education programs, and many analysts believe that increased home sex education would lead to further declines. Of course, even if more parents begin to educate their children about sexuality, the subject will likely still be a part of school health curricula. However, with parents contributing more to the sex education of America's youths, perhaps parents' satisfaction with school sex education programs, which would become strictly supplemental, would increase, and the controversy surrounding such programs abate. The authors in *At Issue: Sex Education* look at several facets of the debate over how sexuality education should be taught to America's youths.

1

The Sex Education Debate: An Overview

Molly Masland

Molly Masland is the health editor for MSNBC.com. Based in Redmond, Washington, she has worked as a producer and reporter for MSNBC, covering a variety of topics from environmental news to Internet crime. She has appeared on MSNBC TV and NBC Nightly News.

The debate over sex education continues amid rising rates of sexually transmitted diseases among teens. Conservatives believe that abstinence education is the best way to address problems associated with teen sex, while liberals endorse comprehensive sex education, which teaches teens how to have safe sex. A middle ground is often achieved when schools stress abstinence but also provide students with information about sexually transmitted diseases and how to prevent them.

Soaring rates of sexually transmitted diseases among teens are adding urgency to the debate over sex education. Conservatives claim the alarming statistics illustrate why abstinence should be the single mantra when it comes to sex ed. Liberals counter that the increase in disease is the strongest case for more detailed information. Caught in the middle are America's kids, who are more vulnerable than ever to potentially deadly diseases.

In the debate over sex education, one thing is undisputed: The average kid today is immersed in sexual imagery. A generation that has grown up on the sordid details of the Starr Report,[1] watched thong-clad teens gyrate on Spring Break cable specials, or read the cover of nearly any women's magazine in the grocery check-out line is familiar with the facts of life.

But young people face a barrage of confusing messages. Along with titillating images from the media, some kids are told to "just say no" to sex. In school, others are taught how to put condoms on bananas in preparation for the real thing, and still other children receive no information whatsoever.

> *Caught in the middle are America's kids, who are more vulnerable than ever to potentially deadly diseases.*

Transcending the cacophony of mixed messages is a host of alarming facts.

Kids are becoming more sexually active at an earlier age. Sixty-six percent of American high school students have had sex by their senior year.

And these same teens are paying the price by contracting dangerous—and sometimes deadly—sexually transmitted diseases [STDs].

According to the Centers for Disease Control and the Kaiser Family Foundation, approximately 65 percent of all sexually transmitted infections contracted by Americans this year will occur in people under 24. One in four new HIV infections occurs in people younger than 22.

"There's a disconnect somewhere. Someone's not getting the message. We need to find out why and help our kids be more responsible," said Dr. Ted Feinberg, assistant executive director of the National Association of School Psychologists.

But what message should be given to young people is the subject of intense debate.

How much to teach?

One side in the debate favors comprehensive sex education, including detailed information about sexually transmitted dis-

---

1. The Starr Report described President Bill Clinton's supposed sexual exploits with White House intern Monica Lewinsky.

eases, contraception and abstinence.

"Young people are going to learn about sex and our question has to be where do we want them to learn? From the media? From their friends? Or do we want them to learn from an educated, responsible adult?" said Tamara Kreinin, president of the Sexuality Information and Education Council of the United States, a leading advocate of comprehensive sex education.

The opposing side pushes for an abstinence-only message that advises teens to wait until marriage.

Since there is no federal law that requires public schools to teach sex education, let alone one that specifies what should be taught, these decisions are left up to states and individual school districts.

Currently 18 states and the District of Columbia require schools to provide sex education and 32 do not. In some states, such as Louisiana, kids might learn about HIV/AIDS, but not about any other STDs or how to prevent pregnancy. In other states, like Washington, teens receive information on everything from birth control pills to homosexuality.

A key issue in the battle over sex education is whether giving kids more information about sex actually leads to sexual activity.

In a study of 35 sex education programs around the world, the World Health Organization found there is no evidence that comprehensive programs encourage sexual activity.

> *In the debate over sex education, one thing is undisputed: The average kid today is immersed in sexual imagery.*

The study also concluded that abstinence-only programs are less effective than comprehensive classes that include abstinence and safe-sex practices such as contraception and condom use.

Related nationwide studies by the Guttmacher Institute and Planned Parenthood came to similar conclusions.

But abstinence-only groups dismiss these studies as biased and skewed. They argue there is a fundamental flaw in giving kids more information about risky behaviors that they should simply be taught to avoid.

"We believe it's an inconsistent message," said Lori Cole,

executive director of the Eagle Forum, a conservative lobby group founded by Phyllis Schlafly. "If you say, 'don't do it, it's not healthy for you, but if you're going to do it, do it this way,' that sends mixed signals to kids."

Cole argues that teaching teens about contraception and STDs only provides "a means for them to live an unhealthy lifestyle."

Looking for a balance

Despite all the disagreement, there is some middle ground in the debate.

Advocates of comprehensive sex education say the abstinence-only message ignores information critical for teens to protect their health. But they are not against the abstinence message itself.

> **With both sides so far apart, there are few signs that a compromise over sex education will be reached anytime soon.**

"Programs in abstinence are very valuable," said Catherine Weiss, director of the ACLU [American Civil Liberties Union's] Reproductive Freedom Project. "It's programs that don't provide any information that we're against. . . . It's as if you're trying to prevent kids from riding motorcycles by forbidding them to wear safety helmets."

Scott Phelps, a researcher and public speaker with the abstinence program Project Reality has heard the arguments of both sides and tried to find a balance.

Project Reality, which provides curriculum and support to districts across Illinois, including 140 public schools in the Chicago area, teaches teens about STDs and contraception, but tries to encourage abstinence by emphasizing the physical and emotional risks of teen sex.

"We recognize the problems of STDs and teen pregnancy, but there are also other risks, such as links to depression and suicide," said Phelps.

Not all comprehensive education proponents are pleased with Project Reality's approach. Some say it puts too much negative spin on sex and may frighten kids. But others say it is at least a step in the right direction.

Parents vs. public schools

While activists argue over the right balance, reports show that American parents want some sort of sex education taught in public schools.

A 1999 survey conducted by Hickman-Brown Research Inc. found that 93 percent of all Americans believe sex education should be taught in high schools, and 84 percent believe it should be taught in middle or junior high schools.

Jodi Hoffman, a Florida mother who successfully sued the Broward County public schools, claiming the district's sex education program was too explicit, represents the minority view among parents. Hoffman said information about sex should only be taught at home, where parents can impart their own values to their children.

She was outraged that the comprehensive sex education classes taught in her three children's schools included information about contraception, abortion and homosexuality.

Hoffman said the courses clash head-on with her religious values. Waiting until marriage to have sex "is the way God intended it to be. That's how it's taught in the Bible and those rules were not written for no reason," said Hoffman.

Fight brews over funding

With both sides so far apart, there are few signs that a compromise over sex education will be reached anytime soon. In fact, the battle is only likely to become more heated. . . .

In 1996, former President [Bill] Clinton signed the Welfare Reform Act, which allocated $250 million over five years to be matched by state dollars—a total of $500 million—for abstinence-only programs. During the first year of the program, 48 states accepted the federal money.

The five-year program expires in 2002 and will once again be up for review. Both sides are revving up for an intense and bitter lobbying effort to lock in future financial support for their agendas.

2

Sex Education Has Failed

Center for AIDS Prevention Studies

The Center for AIDS Prevention Studies (CAPS) at the University of California, San Francisco, conducts research to help prevent HIV infection. CAPS works to stimulate collaboration among researchers, public health professionals, and community-based organizations involved in AIDS prevention efforts.

American teens need accurate information to protect themselves from the dangers of early sexual activity. Conveying scary facts or trying to inflict morals, which is what current sex education programs do, is not working. Moreover, too often in the United States sex education begins in high school, after teens have already become sexually active. Though most sex education programs in the United States are ineffective, some have been successful. Effective programs are those that help teens change their behavior rather than relying an conveying knowledge.

Should sex education be taught in schools?

The question is no longer *should* sex education be taught, but rather *how* should it be taught. Over 93% of all public high schools currently offer courses on sexuality or HIV. More than 510 junior or senior high schools have school-linked health clinics, and more than 300 schools make condoms available on campus. The question now is are these programs effective, and if not, how can we make them better?

Kids need the right information to help protect themselves. The US has more than double the teenage pregnancy rate of any western industrialized country, with more than a million teenagers becoming pregnant each year. Teenagers have the highest rates of sexually transmitted diseases (STDs) of any age group, with one in four young people contracting an STD by the age of 21. STDs, including HIV, can damage teenagers' health and reproductive ability. And there is still no cure for AIDS.

HIV infection is increasing most rapidly among young people. One in four new infections in the US occurs in people younger than 22. In 1994, 417 new AIDS cases were diagnosed among 13–19 year olds, and 2,684 new cases among 20–24 year olds. Since infection may occur up to 10 years before an AIDS diagnosis, most of those people were infected with HIV either as adolescents or pre-adolescents.

Why has sex education failed to help our children?

Knowledge alone is not enough to change behaviors. Programs that rely mainly on conveying information about sex or moral precepts—how the body's sexual system functions, what teens should and shouldn't do—have failed. However, programs that focus on helping teenagers to change their behavior—using role playing, games, and exercises that strengthen social skills—have shown signs of success.

In the US, controversy over what message should be given to children has hampered sex education programs in schools. Too often statements of values ("my children should not have sex outside of marriage") come wrapped up in misstatements of fact ("Sex education doesn't work anyway"). Should we do everything possible to suppress teenage sexual behavior, or should we acknowledge that many teens are sexually active, and prepare them against the negative consequences? Emotional arguments can get in the way of an unbiased assessment of the effects of sex education.

Other countries have been much more successful than the US in addressing the problem of teen pregnancies. Age at first intercourse is similar in the US and five other countries: Canada, England, France, the Netherlands, and Sweden, yet all those countries have teen pregnancy rates that are at least less than half the US rate. Sex education in these other countries is based on the following components: a policy explicitly favoring sex education; openness about sex; consistent messages throughout society; and access to contraception.

Often sex education curricula begin in high school, after many students have already begun experimenting sexually. Studies have shown that sex education begun before youth are sexually active helps young people stay abstinent and use protection when they do become sexually active. The sooner sex education begins, the better, even as early as elementary school.

What kinds of programs work best?

Reducing the Risk, a program for high school students in urban and rural areas in California, used behavior theory–based activities to reduce unprotected intercourse, either by helping teens avoid sex or use protection. Ninth and 10th graders attended 15 sessions as part of their regular health education classes and participated in role playing and experimental activities to build skills and self-efficacy. As a result, a greater proportion of students who were abstinent before the program successfully remained abstinent, and unprotected intercourse was significantly reduced for those students who became sexually active.

> *Age at first intercourse is similar in the US and five other countries . . . yet all those countries have teen pregnancy rates that are at least less than half the US rate.*

Postponing Sexual Involvement, a program for African-American 8th graders in Atlanta, GA, used peers (11th and 12th graders) to help youth understand social and peer pressures to have sex, and to develop and apply resistance skills. A unit of the program also taught about human sexuality, decision-making, and contraceptives. This program successfully reduced the number of abstinent students who initiated intercourse after the program, and increased contraceptive use among sexually experienced females.

Healthy Oakland Teens (HOT) targets all 7th graders attending a junior high school in Oakland, CA. Health educators teach basic sex and drug education, and 9th grade peer educators lead interactive exercises on values, decision-making, communication, and condom-use skills. After one year, students in the program were much less likely to initiate sexual activities such as deep kissing, genital touching, and sexual intercourse.

AIDS Prevention for Adolescents in School, a program for 9th and 11th graders in schools in New York City, NY, focused on correcting facts about AIDS, teaching cognitive skills to appraise risks of transmission, increasing knowledge of AIDS-prevention resources, clarifying personal values, understanding external influences, and teaching skills to delay intercourse and/or consistently use condoms. All sexually experienced students reported increased condom use after the program. A review of 23 studies found that effective sex education programs share the following characteristics:

1. Narrow focus on reducing sexual risk-taking behaviors that may lead to HIV/STD infection or unintended pregnancy.
2. Social learning theories as a foundation for program development, focusing on recognizing social influences, changing individual values, changing group norms, and building social skills.
3. Experimental activities designed to personalize basic, accurate information about the risks of unprotected intercourse and methods of avoiding unprotected intercourse.
4. Activities that address social or media influences on sexual behaviors.
5. Reinforcing clear and appropriate values to strengthen individual values and group norms against unprotected sex.
6. Modeling and practice in communication, negotiation, and refusal skills.

What still needs to be done?

Although sex education programs in schools have been around for many years, most programs have not been nearly as effective as hoped. Schools across the country need to take a rigorous look at their programs, and begin to implement more innovative programs that have been proven effective. Educators, parents, and policy-makers should avoid emotional misconceptions about sex education; based on the rates of unwanted pregnancies and STDs including HIV among teenagers, we can no longer ignore the need for both education on how to post-pone sexual involvement, and how to protect oneself when sexually active. A comprehensive risk prevention strategy uses multiple elements to protect as many of those at risk of pregnancy and STD/HIV infection as possible. Our children deserve the best education they can get.

3

Sex Education Has Succeeded

William R. Finger

William R. Finger writes for Family Health International.

Sex education programs can help teens delay first intercourse and choose to use contraceptives when they do become sexually active. Many studies have shown that educating young adults about sex does not cause them to have sexual relations earlier or increase their sexual activity. Sex education has caused the number of teen pregnancies to drop and reduced teens' risk of sexually transmitted diseases. Giving youths the right information has helped them to make informed decisions about sex.

S ex education can result in young adults delaying first intercourse or, if they are already sexually active, in using contraception. Virtually all studies conclude that sex education does not lead to earlier or increased sexual activity.

"Youth are interested in sex because of biological reasons, hormones," says Dr. Cynthia Waszak, an FHI [Family Health International] senior scientist who focuses on adolescent health. "Suggestions about sex in music, radio, advertisements, films and television reinforce that interest. Kids talk about sex and have questions about it. We should find ways to give youth the right information so they can make better, informed decisions about their sexual behavior."

Learning about reproductive health is part of the larger developmental process as children become adults. Developing self-esteem, a sense of hope and goals for the future, and respect for others are also part of the process. Aspects of education on sexuality are incorporated into various types of programs, sometimes called family life skills or family life education in many developing countries. Married as well as unmarried adolescents need education, on contraception in particular, especially in countries such as Bangladesh and India where 50 to 75 percent of women under age 18 are married.

Sex education programs have been successful in various settings, including schools, community centers, youth groups and the workplace, explains Judith Senderowitz, a U.S.-based consultant who has written extensively on adolescence. The programs often include peer-based approaches and media activities to reach more people. A characteristic of programs that appears critical to success is "an interactive and experiential learning environment where young people can comfortably and safely explore issues and concerns and develop skills to practice safer sexual behavior," reports Senderowitz in one analysis.

Elements for success

Successful sex education programs have common elements that can be adapted to various cultural situations. These common elements include certain features in curriculum and adequate teacher training.

Dr. Douglas Kirby, an analyst for ETR Associates, a U.S.-based educational research company, reviewed sex education programs and found 10 common elements of the most effective programs. Giving a clear, consistent message is critical. "The programs that give the pros and cons to having sex or using condoms and then implicitly say, 'Choose what is best for you,' were not as effective at changing behaviors as the ones that consistently made a specific case. A common effective message was 'always avoid unprotected sex.' Abstinence is the best way—if you have sex, always use a condom."

Making the message appropriate to the age and sexual experience of the participants is also essential. "If few of the participants are having sex, focusing almost entirely on abstinence may be appropriate," he says. The most effective programs concentrated on reducing one or more sexual behaviors that lead to unintended pregnancy or HIV/STD infection.

Another important component, he says, is to identify what should change. "The successful programs," Dr. Kirby says, "all look at the factors that affect sexual behavior—beliefs, attitudes, norms and skills—and design a curriculum to address those factors." Effective programs also provided opportunities for students to practice communication and negotiation skills, and had them personalize the information.

> *Sex education programs have been successful in various settings, including schools, community centers, youth groups and the workplace.*

Traditionally, sex education messages are targeted to one of two groups: those who are sexually active or those who are not. A study suggests that messages could be tailored to address four groups instead: those who do not anticipate having sex in the next year (delayers), those who anticipate initiating sex in the next year (anticipators), those who have had one sexual partner (singles) and those who have had two or more partners (multiples).

As a group, the anticipators showed riskier behaviors and looser ties to family, school and church when compared with the delayers. Youth with multiple sex partners also reported more risks, compared with those who have had only one partner. Health educators should "address the social and psychological context in which sexual experiences occur," recommended researchers from the U.S. Centers for Disease Control and Prevention, which studied 900 students ages 15 to 18 in the United States and Puerto Rico.

Beginning early

The U.S.-based Sexuality Information and Education Council (SIECUS) has developed sex education guidelines. They emphasize beginning early, when children are in primary school, and continuing through adolescence. Teachers need to be trained, and programs should involve the community, parents, administrators and religious leaders. The curriculum should include information on human development, reproductive anatomy, relationships, personal skills, sexual behavior and health, and gender roles.

As countries begin to implement sex education programs, they are drawing to some extent on international guidelines and acknowledged common elements for success. Brazil, for example, has mandated that sex education begin with primary school children. In Mexico, a course developed by the Instituto Mexicano de Investigación de Familia y Población (IMIFAP) called "Planning Your Life" incorporates sex in the larger context of life development. A study by IMIFAP and the New York–based Population Council showed that the course can increase students' knowledge and, among sexually active students, increase contraceptive use.

In Nigeria, a new curriculum emphasizes the development of skills, teacher training and community involvement. A national task force has developed guidelines for comprehensive sex education, working with the SIECUS model. Using the Nigerian guide, the Association for Reproductive and Family Health (ARFH), a Nigerian nongovernmental organization working with the Oyo state government, has developed a curriculum being implemented in 26 schools for 10- to 18-year-olds.

> *As countries begin to implement sex education programs, they are drawing to some extent on international guidelines and acknowledged common elements for success.*

"A needs assessment and baseline survey revealed that, since first sexual experience occurred between ages 13 and 16, youth more than ever before require sexual and reproductive health information as well as some life-building skills—negotiation skills, values clarification, refusal skills, decision-making and goal setting. These skills will enable youth to cope with the demands and challenges of growing up, self-management and other transitions," explains Grace Delano, ARFH executive director. ARFH is also emphasizing training that helps teachers clarify their own values of sexuality. Modifying youths' sexual behavior requires a multidimensional approach, says Delano. "Mass media involvement, advocacy and community involvement are some of the strategies adopted to ensure that the teachings in the school are complemented by the community."

Educators agree on the importance of curricula helping youth to develop and practice decision-making skills. "Sex education is not just about sex," says Hally Mahler, a trainer at

FHI who has facilitated sessions on sex education for teachers, guidance counselors, parents and youth in Asia, Africa and Latin America. "Self-esteem, decision-making skills, feeling you have options and can control things—that is what the curriculum needs to emphasize." For kids to learn skills about negotiating safe sex, teachers have to be comfortable with the content of the curriculum and make it interesting for youth. "We have to get them excited and answer their questions in a real way. So we use music that is popular with kids and exercises that will help people talk about taboo subjects."

One exercise Mahler is incorporating into a new curriculum in Senegal is what she calls a condom fashion show. "Kids, teachers and parents open the condoms and make them into belts, bracelets and earrings. It desensitizes them to this subject, and they can then talk more honestly and openly." Government and nongovernmental organizations are working with FHI to develop the curriculum for use with 10- to 19-year-olds. The Frontiers in Reproductive Health project coordinates this work by the New York–based Population Council.

Little research on sex education among newlyweds exists, and what is available focuses on contraceptive use. China and Bangladesh have used family planning field workers successfully among married adolescents. In Bangladesh, when family planning field workers targeted newlyweds with letters of congratulations and motivational talks, contraception use among newlyweds increased from 19 percent in 1993 to 42 percent in 1997. In Indonesia, counselors use marriage registries to contact newlyweds. Attending talks on family planning is a prerequisite to a civil marriage in several states in Mexico. And in Bangladesh and Taiwan, media campaigns have focused on reaching newlyweds.

Education can help

In the most comprehensive analysis of sex education, the Joint United Nations Programme on HIV/AIDS (UNAIDS) examined 68 evaluations of sex education projects, 53 of which evaluated specific interventions.

Of these 53 interventions, 22 "delayed the onset of sexual activity, reduced the number of sexual partners or reduced unplanned pregnancy and STD [sexually transmitted disease] rates," the UNAIDS analysis concluded. There were neither increases nor decreases in sexual activity and attendant rates of pregnancy and STDs in nearly all of the other interventions evaluated. In one of the few exceptions, a program that included only abstinence in the curriculum resulted in an increase in noncoital sexual activity such as breast touching.

> **//**Most of the successful programs have included strong community involvement and clear messages about avoiding pregnancy or sexually transmitted diseases (STDs).**//**

In the United States, a review of nearly 80 sex education programs also found that "programs that focus upon sexuality, including sex and HIV education programs, school-based clinics, and condom availability programs, do not increase any measure of sexual activity." While nearly all of the programs increased knowledge among youth about sexuality, only a few resulted in measurable reductions in sexual risk-taking, such as delayed onset or reduced frequency of sex, reduced number of sexual partners, or increased use of condoms or other forms of contraception.

Most of the successful programs have included strong community involvement and clear messages about avoiding pregnancy or sexually transmitted diseases (STDs). A study in Senegal found that family life education programs needed to put more emphasis on skill development. The study used focus groups and surveys with 225 boys and girls 14- to 18-years-old who participated in the programs at schools, youth clubs and sports associations. "This [education] allows us to be more mature and to be able to face some of life's problems," said one boy.

The youth also brought up issues involving respect and responsibility. "Discussions about what boys and girls want from each other in relationships suggest a lack of respect between the sexes," the study found. Boys thought that girls were primarily interested in money and other material things from boys, while boys and girls mentioned "the possibility of beatings or rape if a woman refuses to have sexual relations. Values that instill respect for women while teaching that violence is never acceptable need to be emphasized." The Institut de Sciences et l'Environment Université Cheikh Anta Diop de Dakar and FHI conducted the study, working with several ministry offices and nongovernmental organizations.

In a rural, low-income area of the United States, sexual health education for students 5-to 18-years-old involved community agencies, religious leaders, parents, media messages and health promotion. After three years, annual pregnancies fell from 60 to 25 pregnancies per 1,000 young women 14- to 17-years-old. In two control areas with no intervention, annual pregnancies in the same age group increased. The program taught about reproductive anatomy and contraception, and focused on ways to improve decision-making, interpersonal communication skills and self-esteem. It emphasized the need to balance personal values with those of the family, religious institutions and community.

Simply providing educational materials without other key elements, such as community involvement, can be counterproductive. A study in Nicaragua found that placing health education materials in motel rooms used by commercial sex workers actually lowered the frequency of condom use.

Teacher training

Other factors critical for good sex education programs include adequate teacher training and resources for implementing the program. "Training teachers is a key element of successful sex education programs, and the lack of good training has been a big problem," says Dr. Waszak of FHI. "The teachers do not get trained, so they ignore the curriculum or do not know how to deal with it. The training has to desensitize the discomfort the teachers feel in talking about subjects that were taboo when they grew up. And, once you start talking about sexual health with youth, you have to listen to them. You have to deal with their questions, and often, that is not comfortable for teachers."

A recent evaluation of the Peru sex education program suggests the potential limitations of training and resources. "There is still resistance by some teachers asked to implement the program, which undercuts its effectiveness," says Dr. Robert Magnani of Tulane University, who works with FOCUS on Young Adults, a U.S.-based research program. "Not enough time and resources had been committed to gain the support of teachers and principals. This is a big issue in conservative societies."

In South Africa, life-skills training is mandated in all schools by 2005. "But life-skills training curricula and teaching methods vary significantly," says Dr. Magnani. "It is fairly well done in some schools but not done well in others." While recommended national guidelines are important, he says, local provinces have to make financial and other commitments to implement the guidelines.

Good training requires creative approaches. In Jamaica, FHI has worked with the Ministry of Education to train guidance counselors to teach family life skills using a manual called *Preparing for the VIBES in the World of Sexually*. It teaches counselors how to guide youth in developing skits, dances, songs and other theatrical expressions of their questions, concerns, fears and scenarios for sexual situations, working with the Ashe Performing Arts Academy and Ensemble. An evaluation of the program is under way, following for two years youth who participated in the family life skills course at age 12.

The need for good training goes beyond school-based curricula. Involving parents and community leaders is also important. Working in Jamaica with the National Family Planning Board and Ashe, FHI is developing an adolescent reproductive health program for parents. It includes a training manual and video to help parents communicate better with their teenagers. Using the manual, a group of parents will be trained to work with other parents. In an initial needs assessment, about 90 parents expressed concerns about STDs, rape, pregnancy and homosexuality. Reflecting on their own adolescent experiences and concerns for their children, they identified what they thought should go into the manual.

The AIDS epidemic has generated many ways to reinforce sex education messages, including mass media campaigns, hotlines and computers. A campaign in the Philippines targeted young people by using popular music groups and advertising an information hotline. An evaluation of the project found that half of those recalling the music changed their sexual behavior, and 44 percent talked with friends or parents about sex-related information. With the help of young people, the International Planned Parenthood Federation (IPPF) is preparing a Web site with sex education materials. IPPF currently cosponsors a Web site with the BBC World Service called "Sexwise."

Many community organizations have taken an interest in sex education. FHI has worked with the World Association of Girl Guides and Girl Scouts to provide sex education to adolescents in several African countries and India. The Arab-based boy scouts organization has been training youth in peer counseling skills and sensitization about gender and sexual health. In

Ghana, the Young Women's Christian Association is working with the U.S.-based Centre for Development and Population Activities to involve parents and church leaders in counseling.

Peer education programs are particularly popular with HIV-prevention projects. An evaluation of 21 peer-based projects supported by FHI in 10 countries (Brazil, Cameroon, Dominican Republic, Ethiopia, Haiti, Jamaica, Nigeria, Tanzania, Thailand and Zimbabwe) found that 81 percent of the target audience said they preferred getting information on HIV/AIDS from peer educators. A student peer educator in Zimbabwe said, "With someone your own age, you will be serious. You'll feel at ease. With someone older, you do not want to discuss some things, problems, what is in your heart."

4

Abstinence Education Is the Most Effective Way to Protect Teen Health

Robert E. Rector

Robert E. Rector is a senior research fellow in domestic policy studies for the Heritage Foundation. He is the author of America's Failed $5.4 Trillion War on Poverty.

Teen sex is a serious problem that can be significantly reduced with abstinence education programs, which encourage teenagers to delay sexual activity until marriage. Sexually transmitted diseases, emotional and psychological damage, teen pregnancy, and other problems can all result from teen sex. "Safe sex" programs that do not teach abstinence only promote condom use and actually condone teen sexual activity. Abstinence education, in contrast, is effective at reducing early sexual activity among teens. As more funding becomes available for abstinence education, there will be a decrease in teen sexual activity and its attendant ills.

Teenage sexual activity is a major problem confronting the nation and has led to a rising incidence of sexually transmitted diseases (STDs), emotional and psychological injuries, and out-of-wedlock childbearing. Abstinence education programs for youth have been proven to be effective in reducing early sexual activity. Abstinence programs also can provide the foundation for personal responsibility and enduring marital commitment. Therefore, they are vitally important to efforts aimed at reducing out-of-wedlock childbearing among young adult women, improving child well-being, and increasing adult happiness over the long term.

Washington policymakers should be aware of the consequences of early sexual activity, the undesirable contents of conventional "safe sex" education programs, and the findings of the professional literature concerning the effectiveness of genuine abstinence programs. In particular, policymakers should understand that:

- *Sexually transmitted diseases (STDs), including incurable viral infections, have reached epidemic proportions.* Annually, 3 million teenagers contract STDs; STDs afflict roughly one in four teens who are sexually active.
- *Early sexual activity has multiple negative consequences for young people.* Research shows that young people who become sexually active are not only vulnerable to STDs, but also likely to experience emotional and psychological injuries, subsequent marital difficulties, and involvement in other high-risk behaviors.
- *Conventional "safe sex" programs (sometimes erroneously called "abstinence plus" programs) place little or no emphasis on encouraging young people to abstain from early sexual activity.* Instead, such programs strongly promote condom use and implicitly condone sexual activity among teens. Nearly all such programs contain material and messages that would be alarming and offensive to the overwhelming majority of parents.
- *Despite claims to the contrary, there are 10 scientific evaluations showing that real abstinence programs can be highly effective in reducing early sexual activity.* Moreover, real abstinence education is a fairly young field; thus, the number of evaluations of abstinence programs at present is somewhat limited. In the near future, many additional evaluations that demonstrate the effectiveness of abstinence education will become available.

The consequences of early sexual activity

Young people who become sexually active enter an arena of high-risk behavior that leads to physical and emotional damage. Each year, influenced by a combination of a youthful assumption of invincibility and a lack of guidance (or misguidance and misleading information), millions of teens ignore those risks and suffer the consequences.

The nation is experiencing an epidemic of sexually transmitted diseases that is steadily expanding. In the 1960s, the beginning of the "sexual revolution," the dominant diseases related to sexual activity were syphilis and gonorrhea. Today, there are more than 20 widespread STDs, infecting an average of more than 15 million individuals each year. Two-thirds of all STDs occur in people who are 25 years of age or younger. Each year, 3 million teens contract an STD; overall, one-fourth of sexually active teens have been afflicted.

> ***Many young girls report experiencing regret or guilt after their initial sexual experience.*"**

There is no cure for sexually transmitted viral diseases such as the human immunodeficiency virus (HIV) and herpes, which take their toll on people throughout life. Other common viral STDs are the Human Papillomavirus (HPV)—the leading viral STD, with 5.5 million cases reported each year, and the cause of nearly all cases of cervical cancer that kill approximately 4,800 women per year—and Chlamydia trachomatis, which is associated with pelvic inflammatory disease that scars the fallopian tubes and is the fastest growing cause of infertility.

Significantly, research shows that condom use offers relatively little protection (from "zero" to "some") for herpes and no protection from the deadly HPV. A review of the scientific literature reveals that, on average, condoms failed to prevent the transmission of the HIV virus—which causes the immune deficiency syndrome known as AIDS—between 15 percent and 31 percent of the time. It should not be surprising, therefore, that while condom use has increased over the past 25 years, the spread of STDs has likewise continued to rise.

Emotional and psychological injury

Young people who become sexually active are vulnerable to emotional and psychological injury as well as to physical diseases. Many young girls report experiencing regret or guilt after their initial sexual experience. In the words of one psychiatrist who recalls the effects of her own sexual experimentation in her teens, "The longest-standing, deepest wound I gave myself was heartfelt; that sick, used feeling of having given a precious part of myself—my soul—to so many and for nothing, still aches. I never imagined I'd pay so dearly and for so long."

Sexually active youth often live with anxiety about the possibility of an unwanted pregnancy or contracting a devastating STD. Those who do become infected with a disease suffer emotional as well as physical effects. Fears regarding the course of the disease are coupled with a loss of self-esteem and self-confidence. In a survey by the Medical Institute for Sexual Health, 80 percent of those who had herpes said that they felt "less confident" and "less desirable sexually."

In addition, early sexual activity can negatively affect the ability of young people to form stable and healthy relationships in a later marriage. Sexual relationships among teenagers are fleeting and unstable, and broken intimate relationships can have serious long-term developmental effects. A series of broken intimate relationships can undermine an individual's capacity to enter into a committed, loving marital relationship. In general, individuals who engage in premarital sexual activity are 50 percent more likely to divorce later in life than those who do not. Divorce, in turn, leads to sharp reductions in adult happiness and child well-being.

Marital relationships that follow early sexual activity can also suffer from the emotional impact of infertility resulting from an STD infection, ranging from a sense of guilt to depression. In the words of one gynecologist and fertility specialist, "Infertility is so devastating, it often disorients my patients to life itself. This is more than shock or even depression. It impacts every level of their lives, including their marriage."

Teen sex can lead to other high-risk behaviors

Research from a variety of sources indicates a correlation between sexual activity among adolescents and teens and the likelihood of engaging in other high-risk behaviors, such as tobacco, alcohol, and illicit drug use.

A study reported in *Pediatrics* magazine found that sexually active boys aged 12 through 16 are four times more likely to smoke and six times more likely to use alcohol than are those who describe themselves as virgins. Among girls in this same age cohort, those who are sexually active are seven times more likely to smoke and 10 times more likely to use marijuana than are those who are virgins. The report describes sexual activity as a "significant associate of other health-endangering behaviors" and notes an increasing recognition of the interrelation of risk behaviors. Research by the Alan Guttmacher Institute likewise finds a correlation between risk behaviors among adolescents and sexual activity; for example, teenagers who use alcohol, tobacco, and/or marijuana regularly are more likely to be sexually active.

Teen pregnancies

Today, one child in three is born out of wedlock. Only 14 percent of these births occur to women under the age of 18. Most occur to women in their early twenties. Thus, giving birth control to teens in high school through safe-sex programs will have little effect on out-of-wedlock childbearing.

Nearly half of the mothers who give birth outside marriage are cohabiting with the child's father at the time of birth. These fathers, like the mothers, are typically in their early twenties. Out-of-wedlock childbearing is, thus, not the result of teenagers' lack of knowledge about birth control or a lack of availability of birth control. Rather, it is part of a crisis in the relationships of young adult men and women. Out-of-wedlock childbearing, in most cases, occurs because young adult men and women are unable to develop committed, loving marital relationships. Abstinence programs, therefore, which focus on developing loving and enduring relationships and preparation for successful marriages, are an essential first step in reducing future levels of out-of-wedlock births.

Opponents of abstinence education

With millions of dollars in sex-education programs at stake, it is not surprising that the groups that have previously dominated the arena have taken action to block the growing movement to abstinence-only education. Such organizations, including the Sexuality Information and Education Council of the United States (SIECUS), Planned Parenthood, and the National Abortion and Reproductive Rights Action League (NARAL), have been prime supporters of "safe-sex" programs for youth, which entail guidance on the use of condoms and other means of contraception while giving a condescending nod to abstinence. Clearly, the caveat that says "and if you do engage in sex, this is how you should do it" substantially weakens an admonition against early non-marital sexual activity.

Not only do such programs, by their very nature, minimize the abstinence component of sex education, but many of these programs also implicitly encourage sexual activity among the youths they teach. Guidelines developed by SIECUS, for example, include teaching children aged five through eight about masturbation and teaching youths aged 9 through 12 about alternative sexual activities such as mutual masturbation, "outercourse," and oral sex. In addition, the SIECUS guideline suggests informing youths aged 16 through 18 that sexual activity can include bathing or showering together as well as oral, vaginal, or anal intercourse, and that they can use erotic photographs, movies, or literature to enhance their sexual fantasies when alone or with a partner. Not only do such activities carry their own risks for youth, but they are also likely to increase the incidence of sexual intercourse.

In recent years, parental support for real abstinence education has grown. Because of this, many traditional safe-sex programs now take to calling themselves "abstinence plus" or "abstinence-based" education. In reality, there is little abstinence training in "abstinence-based" education. Instead, these programs are thinly disguised efforts to promote condom use. The actual content of most "abstinence plus" curricula would be alarming to most parents. For example, such programs typically have condom use exercises in which middle school students practice unrolling condoms on cucumbers or dildoes.

Abstinence programs

Critics of abstinence education often assert that while abstinence education that exclusively promotes abstaining from premarital sex is a good idea in theory, there is no evidence that such education can actually reduce sexual activity among young people. Such criticism is erroneous. There are currently 10 scientific evaluations (described below) that demonstrate the effectiveness of abstinence programs in altering sexual behavior. Each of the programs evaluated is a real abstinence (or what is conventionally termed an "abstinence only") program; that is, the program does not provide contraceptives or encourage their use.

The abstinence programs and their evaluations are as follows:

1. *Virginity Pledge Programs.* An article in the *Journal of the*

American Medical Association by Dr. Michael Resnick and others entitled "Protecting Adolescents from Harm: Findings from the National Longitudinal Study on Adolescent Health" shows that "abstinence pledge" programs are dramatically effective in reducing sexual activity among teenagers in grades 7 through 12. Based on a large national sample of adolescents, the study concludes that "Adolescents who reported having taken a pledge to remain a virgin were at significantly lower risk of early age of sexual debut."

> *Sexually active boys aged 12 through 16 are four times more likely to smoke and six times more likely to use alcohol than are those who describe themselves as virgins.*

In fact, the study found that participating in an abstinence program and taking a formal pledge of virginity were by far the most significant factors in a youth's delaying early sexual activity. The study compared students who had taken a formal pledge of virginity with students who had not taken a pledge but were otherwise identical in terms of race, income, school performance, degree of religiousness, and other social and demographic factors. Based on this analysis, the authors discovered that the level of sexual activity among students who had taken a formal pledge of virginity was one-fourth the level of that of their counterparts who had not taken a pledge. Overall, nearly 16 percent of girls and 10 percent of boys were found to have taken a virginity pledge.

2. *Not Me, Not Now.* Not Me, Not Now is a community-wide abstinence intervention targeted to 9- to 14-year-olds in Monroe County, New York, which includes the city of Rochester. The Not Me, Not Now program devised a mass communications strategy to promote the abstinence message through paid TV and radio advertising, billboards, posters distributed in schools, educational materials for parents, an interactive Web site, and educational sessions in school and community settings. The program sought to communicate five themes: raising awareness of the problem of teen pregnancy, increasing an understanding of the negative consequences of teen pregnancy, developing resistance to peer pressure, promoting parent-child communica-

tion, and promoting abstinence among teens.

Not Me, Not Now was effective in reaching early teen lis-
teners, with some 95 percent of the target audience within the
county reporting that they had seen a Not Me, Not Now ad.
During the intervention period, the program achieved a statistically significant positive shift in attitudes among pre-teens and
early teens in the county. The sexual activity rate of 15-year-olds
across the county (as reported in the Youth Risk Behavior Survey) dropped by a statistically significant amount from 46.6 percent to 31.6 percent during the intervention period. Finally, the
pregnancy rate for girls aged 15 through 17 in Monroe County
fell by a statistically significant amount, from 63.4 pregnancies
per 1,000 girls to 49.5 pregnancies per 1,000. The teen pregnancy rate fell more rapidly in Monroe County than in comparison counties and in upstate New York in general, and the
difference in the rate of decrease was statistically significant.

3. *Operation Keepsake.* Operation Keepsake is an abstinence
program for 12- and 13-year-old children in Cleveland, Ohio.
Some 77 percent of the children in the program were black or
Hispanic. An evaluation of the program in 2001, involving a
sample of over 800 students, found that "Operation Keepsake
had a clear and sustainable impact on . . . abstinence beliefs."
The evaluation showed that the program reduced the rate of
onset of sexual activity (loss of virginity) by roughly two-thirds
relative to comparable students in control schools who did not
participate in the program. In addition, the program reduced
by about one-fifth the rate of current sexual activity among
those with prior sexual experience.

4. *Abstinence by Choice.* Abstinence by Choice operates in
20 schools in the Little Rock area of Arkansas. The program targets 7th, 8th, and 9th grade students and reaches about 4,000
youths each year. A recent evaluation, involving a sample of
nearly 1,000 students, shows that the program has been highly
effective in changing the attitudes that are directly linked to
early sexual activity. Moreover, the program reduced the sexual
activity rates of girls by approximately 40 percent (from 10.2
percent to 5.9 percent) and the rate for boys by approximately
30 percent (from 22.8 percent to 15.8 percent) when compared
with similar students who had not been exposed to the program. (The sexual activity rate of students in the program was
compared with the rate of sexual activity among control students in the same grade in the same schools prior to the com-
mencement of the program.)

5. *Virginity Pledge Movement.* A 2001 evaluation of the effectiveness of the virginity pledge movement using data from the National Longitudinal Study of Adolescent Health finds that virginity pledge programs are highly effective in helping adolescents to delay sexual activity. According to the authors of the study:

> Adolescents who pledge, controlling for all of the usual characteristics of adolescents and their social contexts that are associated with the transition to sex, are much less likely than adolescents who do not pledge, to have intercourse. The delay effect is substantial and robust. Pledging delays intercourse for a long time.

The study, based on a sample of more than 5,000 students, concludes that taking a virginity pledge reduces by one-third the probability that an adolescent will begin sexual activity compared with other adolescents of the same gender and age, after controlling for a host of other factors linked to sexual activity rates such as physical maturity, parental disapproval of sexual activity, school achievement, and race. When taking a virginity pledge is combined with strong parental disapproval of sexual activity, the probability of initiation of sexual activity is reduced by 75 percent or more.

6. *Teen Aid and Sex Respect.* An evaluation of the Teen Aid and Sex Respect abstinence programs in three school districts in Utah showed that both programs were effective among the students who were at the greatest risk of initiating sexual activity. Approximately 7,000 high school and middle school students participated in the evaluation. To determine the effects of the programs, students in schools with the abstinence programs were compared with students in similar control schools within the same school district. Statistical adjustments were applied to further control for any initial differences between program participants and control students. The programs together were shown to reduce the rate of initiation of sexual activity among at-risk high school students by over a third when compared with a control group of similar students who were not exposed to the program. Statistically significant changes in behavior were not found among junior high students.

When high school and junior high school students were examined together, Sex Respect was shown to reduce the rate of initiation of sexual activity among at-risk students by 25 percent when compared with a control group of similar students who were not exposed to the program. Teen Aid was found to reduce the initiation of sex activity by some 17 percent. A third non-abstinence program, Values and Choices, which offered non-directive or value-free instruction in sex education and decision-making, was found to have no impact on sexual behavior.

7. *Family Accountability Communicating Teen Sexuality (FACTS).* An evaluation performed for the national Title XX abstinence program examined the effectiveness of the Family Account-ability Communicating Teen Sexuality abstinence program in reducing teen sexual activity. The evaluation assessed the FACTS program by comparing a sample of students who participated in the program with a group of comparable students in separate control schools who did not participate in the program. The experimental and control students together comprised a sample of 308 students. The evaluation found the FACTS program to be highly effective in delaying the onset of sexual activity. Students who participated in the program were 30 percent to 50 percent less likely to commence sexual activity than were those who did not participate.

8. *Postponing Sexual Involvement (PSI).* Postponing Sexual Involvement was an abstinence program developed by Grady Memorial Hospital in Atlanta, Georgia, and provided to low-income 8th grade students. A study published in Family Planning Perspectives, based on a sample of 536 low-income students, showed that the PSI program was effective in altering sexual behavior. A comparison of the program participants with a control population of comparable low-income minority students who did not participate showed that PSI reduced the rate of initiation of sexual activity during the 8th grade by some 60 percent for boys and over 95 percent for girls. As the study explained:

> The program had a pronounced effect on the behavior of both boys and girls who had not been sexually involved before the program. . . . By the end of eighth grade, boys who had not had the program were more than three times as likely to have begun having sex as were boys who had the program. . . . Girls who had not had the program were as much as 15 times more likely to have begun having sex as were girls who had had the program.

The effects of the program lasted into the next school year

even though no additional sessions were provided. By the end of the 9th grade, boys and girls who had participated in PSI were still some 35 percent less likely to have commenced sexual activity than were those who had not participated in the abstinence program.

9. *Project Taking Charge.* Project Taking Charge is a six-week abstinence curriculum delivered in home economics classes during the school year. It was designed for use in low-income communities with high rates of teen pregnancy. The curriculum contains these elements: self-development; basic information about sexual biology (anatomy, physiology, and pregnancy); vocational goal-setting; family communication; and values instruction on the importance of delaying sexual activity until marriage. The effect of the program has been evaluated in two sites: Wilmington, Delaware, and West Point, Mississippi. The evaluation was based on a small sample of 91 adolescents. Control and experimental groups were created by randomly assigning classrooms to either receive or not receive the program. The students were assessed immediately before and after the program and through a six-month follow-up.

> *Abstinence education programs have repeatedly been shown to be effective in reducing sexual activity among their participants.*

In the six-month follow-up, Project Taking Charge was shown to have had a statistically significant effect in increasing adolescents' knowledge of the problems associated with teen pregnancy, the problems of sexually transmitted diseases, and reproductive biology. The program was also shown to reduce the rate of onset of sexual activity by 50 percent relative to the students in the control group, although the authors urge caution in the interpretation of these numbers due to the small size of the evaluation sample.

10. *Teen Aid Family Life Education Project.* The Teen Aid Family Life Education Project is a widely used abstinence education program for high school and junior high students. An evaluation of the effectiveness of Teen Aid, involving a sample of over 1,300 students, was performed in 21 schools in California, Idaho, Oregon, Mississippi, Utah, and Washington. The Teen

Aid program was shown to have a statistically significant effect in reducing the rate of initiation of sexual activity (loss of virginity) among high-risk high school students, compared with similar students in control schools. Among at-risk high school students who participated in the program, the rate of initiation of sexual activity was cut by more than one-fourth, from 37 percent to 27 percent. A similar pattern of reduction was found among at-risk junior high school students, but the effects did not achieve statistical significance. The program did not have statistically significant effects among lower-risk students.

How abstinence education helps

Real abstinence education is essential to reducing out-of-wedlock childbearing, preventing sexually transmitted diseases, and improving emotional and physical well-being among the nation's youth. True abstinence education programs help young people to develop an understanding of commitment, fidelity, and intimacy that will serve them well as the foundations of healthy marital life in the future.

Abstinence education programs have repeatedly been shown to be effective in reducing sexual activity among their participants. However, funding for the evaluation of abstinence education programs until very recently has ranged from meager to nonexistent. Currently, the number of adequately funded evaluations of abstinence education is increasing. At present, there are several promising new evaluations nearing completion. As each year passes, it can be expected that the number of evaluations showing that abstinence education does significantly reduce sexual activity will grow steadily.

Abstinence education is a nascent and developing field. Substantial funding for abstinence education became available only within the past few years. As abstinence programs develop and become more broadly available, future evaluations will enable the programs to hone and increase their effectiveness.

5

Most Parents Advocate Abstinence Education for Their Children

The Abstinence Clearinghouse

The Abstinence Clearinghouse is an organization dedicated to promoting an appreciation for and practice of sexual abstinence until marriage through the distribution of age-appropriate, medically referenced materials.

A major survey has found that most parents overwhelmingly oppose comprehensive sex education curricula. Previous polls have indicated parental support for comprehensive sex education, but previous polling has been misleading because the exact nature of what is being taught in comprehensive sex education programs was not clearly defined for parents. The new poll quoted directly from comprehensive sex education curricula, and when faced with this information, the majority of parents disapproved of comprehensive sex education. Most parents prefer that their children learn to abstain from sex until they are married.

A major survey conducted by Zogby International shows that parents overwhelmingly oppose the topics taught to adolescents through comprehensive sex education.

The results of the survey were released today [January 28, 2004] at a press conference in Washington, DC by the Coalition for Adolescent Sexual Health, an ad hoc coalition of groups committed to strong families, research-based education and healthy adolescents.

Polls previously conducted by groups such as Planned Parenthood, Sexuality Information and Education Council of the United States (SIECUS), Advocates for Youth, and the Kaiser Foundation have indicated support by parents for comprehensive sex education. However, members of the Coalition for Adolescent Sexual Health believe that previous polling has been deceptive and illegitimate, because comprehensive sex education has not been adequately defined for parents.

> *In terms of sex education, parents want schools to provide their children with information consistent with their values and expectations.*

Janice Crouse of Concerned Women for America (CWA), a coalition member, states, "Past polls have never really been honest with parents on exactly what comprehensive sex education teaches. Rather than specifically defining comprehensive sex education, questions use generic wording such as, 'Do you support education that prepare adolescents to avoid contracting a deadly sexually transmitted disease?'" "What parents would not answer 'yes' to this question," added Crouse. The supporters of these polls then claim strong support among parents for programs that provide instruction about condoms, according to Crouse.

"We have always believed that parents would reject comprehensive sex education out-of-hand if they only knew what information was being taught to their kids," stated Dr. Bill Maier, a spokesperson for Focus on the Family, a member of the Coalition.

Rather than asking generic questions, the Zogby poll used the specific guidelines for comprehensive sexuality education as developed by SIECUS and the Centers for Disease Control and Prevention and endorsed by such groups as the American Medical Association, American Psychiatric Association, ACLU [American Civil Liberties Union], Planned Parenthood, Human Rights Campaign, People for the American Way, YWCA and more than 90 other groups.

"We did not want to be accused of making things up about comprehensive sex education the way opponents of abstinence education make things up in their polling," said Dr. Maier, "so

we asked Zogby to use verbatim the exact definitions of comprehensive sex education created by its proponents."

In addition to questions based on the comprehensive sex education guidelines, questions were formed using the actual material contained in four of the most widely used comprehensive sex education curricula. "These are not obscure comprehensive sex education curricula, but those programs the CDC [Centers for Disease Control] has most actively recommended for years," added Maier.

As a contrast to comprehensive sex education, parents were also asked their level of support for the guidelines of abstinence-plus-character education. According to Genevieve Wood, spokesperson for the Family Research Council, "At last we have a survey that settles the question on what parents think of different types of sex education. The Zogby poll asked parents straight-up questions that did not spin either comprehensive sex education or abstinence education into something other than they are."

The results

In total, 1245 parents (random sample, margin of error = 2.8%) were asked 29 questions about sex education—7 questions dealing with abstinence education, 14 general questions dealing with comprehensive sex education (sometimes erroneously called "abstinence-first" or "abstinence-plus-condoms" education), 5 questions dealing with CDC-promoted sex education curricula and 3 questions dealing with miscellaneous aspects of comprehensive sex education.

Following are the results:

	% of parents who approve or strongly approve	% of parents who disapprove or strongly disapprove
Comprehensive sex education guidelines	25.4%	60.5%
Abstinence education guidelines	73.4%	15.8%
CDC-promoted sex education curricula	14.2%	74.9%
Misc. aspects of condom-based "safer-sex" education	22.5%	68.0%

By a 2.4 to 1 margin, parents disapprove or strongly disapprove sex education.

By a 4.9 to 1 margin, parents disapprove or strongly disapprove of the information contained in CDC-promoted sex education curricula.

According to Crouse of CWA, "The message is clear. Parents want the best for their children. In terms of sex education, parents want schools to provide their children with information consistent with their values and expectations. Parents want their children to receive a strong message on abstinence. The overwhelming proportion of parents disapprove of the messages contained in comprehensive or "safer-sex" education."

Leslee Unruh, president of the National Abstinence Clearinghouse, another coalition member, agrees. "This report proves once and for all what parents really think. They do not want strangers and teachers telling their children *how* to have sex. Parents want their children taught about responsibility, decision making, healthy choices and how to build a long lasting marriage relationship. Teaching kids how to use a condom accomplishes none of these objectives. Abstinence-until-marriage education that follows the federal definition set up in the welfare reform legislation is what parents want."

6

Advocates of Abstinence Education Are Hypocrites

Sarah Goff

Sarah Goff was a sophomore at Yale University when this viewpoint was written.

Those who support abstinence-only education are hypocritical. It is easy for people to claim that, where the question of teen sex is concerned, abstinence is the only acceptable choice when they are no longer young and likely made different choices when they were. Policy makers should keep in mind the fact that abstinence education is not something they would have wanted when they were teenagers. Their need to impose morality should not attempt to override the realities of being a teenager.

Some people played drinking games. Others ignored it entirely. As for me, during this year's State of the Union Address, I sat alone in my suitemate's room and screamed at her television. Yes, that was me yelling, "Abstinence-only education? Suck it, you hypocrite!"

Al Franken has done an excellent job of pointing out the hypocrisy of abstinence as a form of sex education in public schools, as he did in his fabulous *Lies and the Lying Liars Who Tell Them: A Fair and Balanced Look at the Right*. Franken extended an invitation to many prominent figures in the George W. Bush . . . administration, including George W. himself, to share their stories of struggle and triumph growing up as teenagers who abstained from sex. Their responses were to be published in a book he claimed he was writing called *Savin' It!* Needless to say, he has received no responses.

Why is it best to frame the debate this way? It offers the most insightful criticism into the deceptive argument put forth by those who promote abstinence-only education. Assuming perfect adherence to a "contraceptive method," if you could call abstinence such a thing, abstinence is better than all other contraceptive methods. It is perfectly effective at preventing the transmission of STDs [sexually transmitted diseases] and AIDS and, excepting the holy virgin, has never failed at preventing pregnancy. This is exactly how Bush and other supporters of abstinence-only education have presented the issue, as he did in his [2004] State of the Union Address.

> *It is very easy to say that abstinence is the only contraceptive method for young people when you personally are not young and when you were, you did not abstain.*

Of course, this argument is similar to saying that the best way to prevent head injuries related to riding a bicycle is to never ride a bike at all. Well, never until marriage that is. Here's the problem: Our parents all rode bicycles at some point when they were young. They probably did so before they were old enough to ride safely, by watching out for cars and only riding in daylight. They did it anyway. Some of them fell over and some of them did not, but those who wore helmets protected themselves from massive head injuries. So, imagine that you are a kid again . . . being told by the very people whom you know rode bicycles at your age that you are not allowed to ride one or even to learn what a helmet is. The word I think we are all looking for now is hypocrisy.

Decision makers are far from their teen years

It is very easy to say that abstinence is the only contraceptive method for young people when you personally are not young and when you were, you did not abstain. But even if those who are in favor of abstinence-only education did abstain from sex, it still does not mean that abstinence is a viable or attractive option for most unmarried people today. In fact, I would argue that promoting a culture of abstinence with regard to both bicycles and sex is undesirable. Kids who want to should be able to ride bicycles, provided that they wear helmets. Bicycle-riding is a valuable part of life and growing up, and I would hope that we could all agree that riding bikes is fun. The same goes for mature teenagers who want to have sex. The current stress on the need for 100 percent safety is paranoid or dishonest. Clearly, it would be better to eliminate elements of paranoia and dishonesty in our attitudes about sex than to incorporate them into public policy.

I could see how people might choose to overlook these problems, were it the case that abstinence-only education had been definitively proven to reduce incidences of unwanted pregnancy or STDs and HIV/AIDS. However, a report published by NARAL (National Abortion and Reproductive Rights Action League) argued that, "Abstinence programs have not been proven effective and may result in riskier behavior by teenagers. Responsible sex education programs, on the other hand, have demonstrated positive results such as delayed initiation of sex, reduced frequency of sex, and increased contraceptive use." Super. So why does Bush want to increase funding for abstinence-only education to $2 billion, as he said in his Presidential Address?

> **//** *Clearly, it would be better to eliminate elements of paranoia and dishonesty in our attitudes about sex than to incorporate them into public policy.* **//**

Much of the research done on the efficacy of abstinence-only education relies on short-term data, such as the number of teenagers who have signed pledges to abstain from sex. Very little research has been done on actual, long-term results and there have been no nationwide or large-scale studies that I have heard of on the subject. In fact, in 2001, the National Campaign to Prevent Teen Pregnancy "found no credible studies of abstinence-only programs showing any significant impact on participants' initiation of or frequency of sex." I would also be curious to know how these studies are actually operated—information that is not made readily available to the public. Do they consist of an adult authority figure asking teenagers every month or so, "Have you had sex yet? Have you lied and broken your abstinence-pledge? Are you planning on disappointing us soon?"

Data on abstinence-only education is weak

But not surprisingly, the push for abstinence-only education does not actually rest on data about efficacy. Advocates for abstinence-only programs rely instead on discussing the problems of sending "mixed messages" to teenagers. They fret about the emotional risks associated with sex. They point to the relatively high failure rate of condoms among new users, as high as 15 percent over the course of one year in some studies. Of course, this last problem is exactly what more comprehensive sex-education advocates would like to improve by providing information about effective contraceptive use.

Would advocates of abstinence-only education have accepted such arguments about teenage immaturity when they were themselves teenagers? No one should be forced to be kept ignorant, when such information offers a wider range of life choices. Policy-makers need to consider the facts and the people they are supposedly trying to help rather than only their own morality and commit to a more effective system of education than one based purely on abstinence-only policies.

7

Comprehensive Sex Education Is the Most Effective Way to Protect Teen Health

John P. Elia

John P. Elia is a faculty member in the departments of health education and psychology at San Francisco State University. His research interests include the history and philosophy of sexuality education in the United States, sexual prejudice, and health promotion. He is the editor of If You Seduce a Straight Person, Can You Make Them Gay? *and* Readings in Comprehensive Sexuality, *portions of which are adapted in this viewpoint.*

Many students will engage in sexual relationships, as evidenced by the high number of unintended teen pregnancies that occur annually. To help youths avoid problems associated with sex, comprehensive sexuality education teaches students how to have sex responsibly. Being well educated about sex can help teens avoid pregnancy and sexually transmitted diseases, foster healthy relationships, and be prepared for problems such as sexual harassment and rape. Age-appropriate lessons in sexuality should occur early in the primary grades and become more specific and sophisticated as students reach middle and high school. Also important is preparing teachers to discuss sexual topics openly with students and treat sexual diversity respectfully.

John P. Elia, "The Necessity of Comprehensive Sexuality Education in Schools," *The Educational Forum*, vol. 64, Summer 2000. Copyright © 2000 by *The Educational Forum*. Reproduced by permission of Kappa Delta Pi, International Honor Society in Education.

For more than a century, public schools have had a limited approach to sexuality education. At best, instruction has been limited to lessons about the sexual anatomy, reproductive physiology, and sexually transmitted diseases (STDs). A more comprehensive sexuality education—one that addresses biomedical, cultural, ethical, and psychological aspects of sexuality—has been conspicuously absent in more than 90 percent of schools nationwide. . . .

Traditional notions and practices

Sexuality education has never enjoyed much prominence in U.S. primary and secondary schools. Nor has it reflected the complexity of human sexuality. Sexuality education began in the United States during the late-19th and early-20th centuries to combat STDs and teach sexual morality and propriety to the young. Physical education teachers were responsible for teaching sexuality education—not because they had special training but because usually the only time during the school day when students were segregated by sex was in gym class. Having gym teachers teach sexuality education symbolically linked sexuality solely to the physical aspects of life and reinforced the notion that sexuality was a physical thing, frequently foreclosing exploration of broader issues.

The legacy of educating students about the biomedical and hygienic aspects of sexuality has survived up to the present. Health educators and biology teachers often have been responsible for sexual instruction. Restricting sexuality education to these curricula limits and biases the educational experience toward mechanical and disease-related aspects, again reducing sexuality to a physical phenomenon.

During the 1980s and '90s—with the advent of the Adolescent Family Life Act of 1981 and a welfare reform bill of 1996—the federal government for the first time formally endorsed abstinence-only sexuality education. As Daley has indicated, abstinence-only sexuality education explicitly states that:
  • there are social, psychological, and health advantages of abstaining from sexual activity until married;
  • the only way to prevent out-of-wedlock pregnancy and STDs is by sexual abstinence;
  • monogamy within the context of marriage is the socially expected standard for sexual conduct;
  • sexual expression outside of marriage will probably have

detrimental mental and physical effects; and

• having a child out-of-wedlock often has deleterious effects on the child.

Though supporters have made additional claims regarding the positive effects of the abstinence-only approach, these statements capture its generally restrictive spirit. It may never be articulated by sexuality educators, yet students leave the classroom with an understanding that heterosexuality is more revered and is simply better than other sexual identities and lifestyles. Discussions about bisexuality and homosexuality rarely occur in the classroom. Essentially, this approach conveys the message that bisexuals, gays, and lesbians are not "fully sexual human beings" and that their sexuality is downright wrong. Bisexual, gay, and lesbian students are not the only ones negatively impacted by such an approach. Because of the strong emphasis on marriage, those heterosexuals who choose not to marry are made to feel like social misfits and failures. After all, students often are taught with the assumption that they will eventually settle down into a heterosexually based, monogamous, nuclear family and produce children. Additionally, traditional sexuality education programs seldom question conventional gender roles, sexual prejudice, sexism, and basic assumptions about traditional views of sexuality in general.

> *Comprehensive sexuality education is* inclusive, *whereas traditional and abstinence-only approaches are* exclusive.

Besides teaching about the physiological, mechanical aspects of sexuality along with the prevailing abstinence-only message, Haffner noted, some courses present a "hidden curriculum" that "teaches teenagers that in order to be popular, one has to be attractive, physically fit and able-bodied, heterosexual, conform to gender-role expectations, and dress according to school norms." Much of the current curricula give students the impression that sexual expression is reserved for adults; minors engaging in sexual activities are "playing with fire." Fluidity of sexual expression, the language of sexual intimacy, and the creativity of human sexual response are sorely missing in traditional sexuality education programs.

Comprehensive sexuality education

Comprehensive sexuality education is *inclusive*, whereas traditional and abstinence-only approaches are *exclusive*. Essentially, the former involves covering a wide variety of topics and perspectives, including abstinence, as possibilities. In part, comprehensive sexuality education focuses on both the positive and negative consequences of sexual activity. According to Yarber, "The comprehensive approach not only deals with traditional areas such as reproductive biology and puberty, dating, marriage, and STD[s], but also covers many topics historically considered inappropriate, such as sexual pleasure, noncoital sexual expression, sexuality and society, and homosexuality." SIECUS [Sexuality Information and Education Council of the United States] has urged that comprehensive sexuality education should encompass "sexual development, reproductive health, interpersonal relationships, affection, intimacy, body image, and gender roles." SIECUS added that sexuality education should address biological, sociocultural, psychological, and spiritual dimensions of sexuality, drawing "from the cognitive domain (information); the affective domain (feelings, values, and attitudes); and behavioral domain (communication, decisionmaking, and other relevant personal skills)." As SIECUS concluded,

> Comprehensive school-based sexuality education that is appropriate to students' age, developmental level, and cultural background should be an important part of the education program at every age. A comprehensive sexuality education program respects the diversity of values and beliefs represented in the community and will complement and augment the sexuality education children receive from their families.

This approach more faithfully reflects the complexity and multidimensionality of sexuality.

Perhaps one of the most salient features of comprehensive sexuality education is its commitment to the needs and concerns of students. Because of the myriad aspects of sexuality, it is impossible to address them all in one class. It should be taught across the curriculum and not face the limitations of health and biological studies. As Carlson argued, sexuality education must become "critical and analytical and thus more personally and socially empowering."

Why teach about sexuality?

Sexuality education belongs in the schools. Individuals deserve to know about the multifaceted aspects of this important part of their lives. Because sexuality is such a controversial topic, however, less than ten percent of K–12 children in the nation receive comprehensive sexuality education. Furthermore, many teenagers report that the sexuality education they have received in school is inadequate and "frequently at odds with what . . . they want to know in terms of sexuality and relationships."

Students should have opportunities to study sexuality, choosing aspects of sexuality or topics that they find relevant to their lives or intriguing. Students enrolling in courses such as biology, literature, health, history, psychology, or social studies could pursue topics in human sexuality that interest them. They could undertake projects with teachers' guidance. Because students should be afforded some choice of studies, the school board, school administrators, teachers, counselors, librarians, and parents or guardians must support freedom of inquiry and encourage students to undertake high-quality projects or have experiences that would have real value for them. This freedom of inquiry is at the heart of democratic ideals. In many ways, it is the opposite of the censorship that, as Scales suggested, is infiltrating our educational system at an ever-quickening pace and is threatening our freedom at the constitutional level.

Broadly based sexuality education should be taught to foster the quality of life for students and individuals in general. Sexuality runs through the very fabric of social life. It is important to help students become sexually self-aware, as they explore their own sexuality and develop intimate and sexual relationships. Though many in the school community argue that students are not or should not be sexual, students often engage in sexual relationships. If children or adolescents are not sexual, why do more than one million unintended teenage pregnancies occur annually in the United States? Furthermore, 40 percent of ninth-graders and 45 percent of tenth-graders have engaged in sexual intercourse—and once they have engaged in this activity they are likely to repeat the experience.

Psychologists and counselors agree that sexually intimate relationships are one of the most important and cherished aspects of our lives. Though a clear majority of children report having had a boyfriend or girlfriend, few people receive education in the area of sex and relationships. Healthy relationships add immeasurably to the quality of life and should be an integral part of schooling.

Sexuality education should occur early in the primary grades, and teachers should always strive to make it age appropriate. Basic, fundamental information should be handled very broadly and simply in the primary grades and then become more specific and sophisticated in middle and high school.

Noting that literature teachers are often inspired and encouraged to teach students the love of literature, Passmore, asked, "Why are teachers in general not encouraged to teach students the love of other people?" As Passmore suggested, sexuality education should be taught to destroy myths about sexuality, assist students in making decisions about their sexuality, and, finally, prepare them "for love, with its joys, its responsibilities."

Acquiring these skills would help students manage intimate/sexual relationships. Furthermore, many of these skills are likely to be transferable to other aspects of students' lives. For example, communication and conflict-resolution techniques can be applied to relationships with employers, friends, relatives, lovers or sex partners, and others.

> *Perhaps one of the most salient features of comprehensive sexuality education is its commitment to the needs and concerns of students.*

Additionally, sexuality educations could be expected to help reduce the incidence of sexual harassment, sexual coercion, and rape. These crimes are far too common to be ignored in the education of the young. Statistically, one in four women will face rape—a conservative estimate, given that the report rate is low. Approximately 85 percent of rapes are committed by dates or acquaintances, and the individuals who get raped are reluctant to press criminal charges against people they know or care about. Sexually education could be enormously helpful in making clear the issues associated with sexual consent and in teaching rape prevention.

Because sexuality is an important aspect of most people's lives, sexuality education would be beneficial in promoting positive mental and physical health. Many people feel negatively about sexuality because of how it has been portrayed by religious and biomedical writers. Consequently, conversations about sexuality usually occur behind closed doors in a secretive fashion; in many cases, sexual partners do not even discuss sexual matters. Sexuality education would be instrumental in "normalizing" and depathologizing sexuality. Without sexuality education, many people will likely continue to feel badly about their own sexuality and about sexuality in general.

Perhaps the best reason for teaching sexuality education in schools is because it is likely to be relevant to students' lives. So much of what is taught in schools today is presented unimaginatively; worse, it is often disconnected from students' lives. Sexuality will capture the interest of students because it is central to most of their lives. Most students want to date or carry on some type of romantic involvement. Numerous surveys have indicated that most adolescents desire sexuality education.

Many children and adolescents learn about sexuality on the streets, picking up incorrect and inadequate information. The mass media also dispense inadequate information. Brown, Childers, and Waszak reported that adolescents view between 1,900 and 2,400 sexually related images on television annually. Many of these messages are contradictory and confusing. Yet these minors have no real way of discussing the meanings and implications of the images they see with anyone other than friends, who know little more than they do, perpetuating misinformation.

Sexuality education in the schools would necessarily have to address various sexual lifestyles, sexual values, belief systems, and forms of sexual expression. This form of education would thus be an effective vehicle to study and practice democratic ideals. Through monitored controversy, dissent, debate, critical deliberation, and questioning, students would be afforded a firsthand experience of what it means to be in a pluralistic society and work out problems and concerns in a socially rich environment. To pretend that these differences do not exist is unfair to students, who will eventually find themselves outside the school walls with individuals possessing a variety of beliefs and practices regarding sexual and social relationships. Furthermore, to ignore such differences is unfair to students who differ from the "norm," for they will remain invisible and unappreciated.

Much prejudice is directed at those who do not display "normal" sexual or gender behaviors. Bisexuals, gays, lesbians, or those who simply do not fit typical gender-role stereotypes are discriminated against and physically and verbally abused in the schools. As Ginsberg noted, "Our societal values categorize homosexuality as deviant, sinful, or both, and our schools are populated by adolescent peers and adult educators who share these heterosexual values." Sexuality education could address discrimination, encouraging tolerance if not acceptance of these people by using a democratic educational framework and emphasizing justice, equity, freedom for all, and protection of minority rights—another opportunity to explore the nature of democracy.

Though the Gay, Lesbian, Straight, Education Network, the Gay-Straight Alliance, and other groups have improved the quality of school life for queer-identified youth, we must address issues of bisexuality and homosexuality across the curriculum. Queer youth have an extremely difficult time in school, which has, in part, led to school failure, drug abuse, suicide and attempted suicide, and other undesirable consequences.

On a more positive note, Steutel and Spieker have suggested that *good* sex should be both the aim of sexuality education and a chief reason why it ought to be offered. They referred to "good" in both moral and non-moral ways. Morally, they referred to the types of sexuality that can withstand moral criticism. In other words, such issues as consent, keeping one's integrity intact, and being mindful of one's and others' physical and emotional well-being are a part of morally good sex. In a non-moral sense, good involves the pleasurable, gratifying, and generally enjoyable sexual encounters that lead to being fulfilled. For Steutel and Spieker, both the moral and non-moral aspects of *good* sex must be integral in sexuality education aiming at personal growth and happiness.

Necessary conditions

A requisite condition for offering comprehensive sexuality education is to articulate a philosophy of education that accommodates the complexities of this educational enterprise. An appropriate philosophy of education would be compatible with and espouse democratic ideals. As Sears asserted, "Public schools in a democratic society are a marketplace for ideas." Access to these ideas, as Justice Brennan wrote, "prepares students for active and effective participation in the pluralistic, often contentious society in which they will soon be adult members." A practical and socially responsible philosophy of education must form the foundation for a responsive and solid sexuality education curriculum.

Our society should run its public educational system on democratic ideals. The spirit of such an educational enterprise ought to pay serious attention to and embrace an educational philosophy that deals with representation, dissent, controversy, justice, fairness, respect for diversity, freedom of speech, equality, choice, and consent. As Noddings noted, "To achieve a democracy we must try things out, evaluate them without personal prejudice, revise them if they are found wanting, and decide what to do next through a process of reasoned consensus or compromise in which authority of expertise is consulted but not allowed to impose its views with no discussion of how, why, and on what grounds." According to Sears, "The educator has an important role in a democratic society: to encourage intellectual flexibility, to foster analytical thought, and to expand tolerance." Yet professional educators at the primary, secondary, and even post-secondary levels have often failed to fulfill the role that Noddings and Sears have outlined, both in the standard curriculum and in sexuality education.

> *Sexuality education, in particular, suffers from censorship, dilution of material and information, and outright bigotry.*

Arnstine asserted that schools are undemocratic, painting a rather bleak picture of authoritarian schooling conditions. As Arnstine noted, "The system's purpose is to support and help maintain the status quo of our dominant social institutions, which are hierarchical, authoritarian, and unequal, competitive, racist, sexist, and homophobic. It achieves this purpose by keeping the young in school under adult surveillance as long as possible." Progressive educators oppose such educational methods, encouraging students toward self-governance. These child-centered or society-centered educators are sensitive to children's needs and interests.

Yet schooling has been neither democratic nor student centered. Sexuality education, in particular, suffers from censorship, dilution of material and information, and outright bigotry. In many cases, teachers are told what they can and cannot

teach because it is an area of contested values. Given the hege-
monic status of the Far Right (as exemplified in the abstinence-
only approach), currently financially supported by the U.S.
government, it is no wonder sexuality education is undemocratic. If students ask questions or pursue issues that fall outside
of the purview of what is permitted in the curriculum, their inquiries are usually ignored summarily or pushed aside.

Though a complete treatment of all of the conditions necessary for comprehensive sexuality education to be integrated
in the schools is not possible here, the following suggestions
may make this type of sexuality education possible. First, the
school must establish a curriculum based on democratic prin-
ciples. Second, teachers must be open to the concerns and
issues of students, avoiding sexuality education based on ideologies, whether abstinence-only or permissive. Third, participants must improve student and teacher relationships through
respect, trust, caring, empathy, and open communication.
Fourth, teacher education programs must prepare teachers to
discuss sexual matters in the classroom. Fifth, students and
teachers must work conjointly to solve problems emerging
from inquiries, which will result in reflective and active think-
ing. Sixth, participants must treat diversity as a necessary condition for learning rather than a liability. Finally, administrators must restructure the school environment to obliterate
authoritarianism; this step will also require major efforts at the
federal, state, and district levels.

Meeting the need

Comprehensive sexuality is greatly needed. Developing this
approach will allow schools to enhance the quality of education and of life in general. This goal can only be reached if traditional notions about, and practices of, sexuality education
are challenged. We must replace these limiting learning approaches with a more encompassing sexuality education based
on democratic ideals.

8

Comprehensive Sex Education Does Not Work

Kerby Anderson

Kerby Anderson is the national director of Probe Ministries International and the author of several books, including Living Ethically in the '90s *and* Moral Dilemmas. *He also served as general editor for* Marriage, Family, and Sexuality *and* Technology, Spirituality, & Social Trends. *He is a nationally syndicated columnist and frequently serves as guest host on* Point of View *on the USA Radio Network.*

Teaching comprehensive sex education, handing out condoms to teens, and establishing community clinics are not effective in reducing teen sexual activity and pregnancies. Teaching teens about the mechanics of sex without informing them of the moral and psychological implications of engaging in sex merely encourages teens to experiment sexually. Indeed, sex education can increase the knowledge teens have about human sexuality, but it does not shape their sexual behavior in a positive way. Teaching teens to abstain from sex is the best way to protect their health and well-being.

For more than thirty years proponents of comprehensive sex education have argued that giving sexual information to young children and adolescents will reduce the number of unplanned pregnancies and sexually transmitted diseases [STDs]. In that effort nearly $3 billion have been spent on federal Title X family planning services; yet teenage pregnancies and abortions rise.

Perhaps one of the most devastating popular critiques of comprehensive sex education came from Barbara Dafoe Whitehead. The journalist . . . was willing to say that sex education was wrong. Her article, "The Failure of Sex Education" in *Atlantic Monthly*, demonstrated that sex education neither reduced pregnancy nor slowed the spread of STDs.

Comprehensive sex education is mandated in at least seventeen states, so Whitehead chose one of those states and focused her analysis on the sex education experiment in New Jersey. Like other curricula the New Jersey sex education program rests on certain questionable assumptions.

The first tenet is that children are "sexual from birth." Sex educators reject the classic notion of a latency period until approximately age twelve. They argue that you are "being sexual when you throw your arms around your grandpa and give him a hug."

Second, children are sexually miseducated. Parents, to put it simply, have not done their job, so we need "professionals" to do it right. Third, if miseducation is the problem, then sex education in the schools is the solution. Parents are failing miserably at the task, so "it is time to turn the job over to the schools. Schools occupy a safe middle ground between Mom and MTV."

Learning About Family Life is the curriculum used in New Jersey. While it discusses such things as sexual desire, AIDS, divorce, and condoms, it nearly ignores such issues as abstinence, marriage, self-control, and virginity.

> *Contrary to claims by sex educators, condom education does not significantly change sexual behavior.*

Whitehead concludes that comprehensive sex education has been a failure. For example, the ratio of teenage births to unwed mothers was 67 percent in 1980 and rose to 84 percent in 1991. In the place of this failed curriculum, Whitehead describes a better program. She found that "sex education works best when it combines clear messages about behavior with strong moral and logistical support for the behavior sought."

One example she cites is the Postponing Sexual Involvement program at Grady Memorial Hospital in Atlanta, Georgia, which offers more than a "Just say no" message. It reinforces the message by having adolescents practice the desired behavior and enlists the aid of older teenagers to teach younger teenagers how to resist sexual advances. Whitehead also found that "religiously observant teens" are less likely to experiment sexually, thus providing an opportunity for church-related programs to help stem the tide of teenage pregnancy.

What about condoms?

Are condoms a safe and effective way to reduce pregnancy and STDs? Sex educators seem to think so. Every day sex education classes throughout this country promote condoms as a means of safe sex or at least safer sex. But the research on condoms provides no such guarantee.

For example, Texas researcher Susan Weller, writing in the journal. *Social Science Medicine*, evaluated all research published on condom effectiveness. She reported that condoms are only 87 percent effective in preventing pregnancy and 69 percent effective in reducing the risk of HIV infection. This 69 percent effectiveness rate is also the same as a 31 percent failure rate in preventing AIDS transmission.

To be effective, condoms must be used "correctly and consistently." Most individuals, however, do not use them "correctly and consistently" and thus get pregnant and get sexually transmitted diseases.

Contrary to claims by sex educators, condom education does not significantly change sexual behavior. An article in the *American Journal of Public Health* stated that a year-long effort at condom education in San Francisco schools resulted in only 8 percent of the boys and 2 percent of the girls using condoms every time they had sex.

Even when sexual partners use condoms, sometimes condoms fail. Most consumers do not know that the FDA [Food and Drug Administration] quality-control standards allow for a maximum failure rate of four per 1,000 using a water fill test. And even if condoms are used correctly, do not break, and do not leak, they are still far from 100 percent effective. The Medical Institute for Sexual Health reported that "medical studies confirm that condoms do not offer much, if any, protection in the transmission of chlamydia and human papillomavirus, two serious STDs with prevalence as high as 40 percent among sexually active teenagers."

Nevertheless, condoms have become the centerpiece of U.S. AIDS policy and the major recommendation of most sex education classes in America. Many sex educators have stopped calling their curricula "safe sex" and have renamed them "safer sex"—focusing instead on various risk reduction methods. But is this false sense of security and protection actually increasing the risks young people face?

If kids buy the notion that if they just use condoms they will be safe from AIDS or any other sexually transmitted disease whenever they have sex, they are being seriously misled. They should be correctly informed that having sex with any partner having the AIDS virus is life-threatening, condoms or no condoms. It would be analogous to playing Russian roulette with two bullets in your six chambers. Using condoms removes only one of the bullets. The gun still remains deadly with the potential of a lethal outcome.

School-based health clinics

As comprehensive sex education curricula have been promoted in the schools, clinics have been established to provide teens greater access to birth control information and devices. Proponents cite studies that supposedly demonstrate the effectiveness of these clinics on teen sexual behavior. Yet a more careful evaluation shows that school-based health clinics do not lower the teen pregnancy rate.

The most often-cited study involved the experience of the clinic at Mechanics Arts High School in St. Paul, Minnesota. Researchers found that a drop in the number of teen births during the late 1970s coincided with an increase in female participation at the school-based clinic. But at least three important issues undermine the validity of this study.

First, some of the statistics are anecdotal rather than statistical. School officials admitted that the schools could not document the decrease in pregnancies. Second, the total female enrollment of the two schools included in the study dropped significantly. Third, the study actually shows a drop in the teen birth rate rather than the teen pregnancy rate. The reduction in the fertility rate listed in the study was likely due to more teenagers obtaining an abortion.

Today, more and more advocates of school-based health clinics are citing a three-year study headed by Laurie Zabin at Johns Hopkins University, which evaluated the effect of sex education on teenagers. The study of two school-based clinics in Baltimore, Maryland, showed there was a 30 percent reduction in teen pregnancies.

> *If kids buy the notion that if they just use condoms they will be safe from AIDS or any other sexually transmitted disease whenever they have sex, they are being seriously misled.*

But even this study leaves many unanswered questions. The size of the sample was small and over 30 percent of the female sample dropped out between the first and last measurement periods. Critics point out that some girls who dropped out of the study may have dropped out of school because they were pregnant. Other researchers point out that the word *abortion* is never mentioned in the brief report, leading them to conclude that only live births were counted.

On the other hand, an extensive, national study done by the Institute for Research and Evaluation shows that community-based clinics used by teenagers actually increase teen pregnancy. A two-year study by Joseph Olsen and Stan Weed found that teenage participation in these clinics lowered teen birth rates. But when pregnancies ending in miscarriage or abortion were factored in, the total teen pregnancy rates increased by as much as 120 pregnancies per one thousand clients.

Douglas Kirby, former director of the Center for Population Options, had to admit the following: "We have been engaged in a research project for several years on the impact of school-based clinics. . . . We find basically that there is no measurable impact upon the use of birth control, not upon pregnancy rates or birth rates."

Sex education programs

As we've seen, the evidence indicates that the so-called "solution" provided by sex educators can actually make problems worse.

The problem is simple: education is not the answer. Teaching comprehensive sex education, distributing condoms, and establishing school-based clinics is not effective. When your audience is impressionable teens entering puberty, explicit sex education does more to entice than educate. Teaching them the "facts" about sex without providing any moral framework merely breaks down mental barriers of shame and innocence and encourages teens to experiment sexually.

A Louis Harris poll conducted for Planned Parenthood found that the highest rates of teen sexual activity were among those who had comprehensive sex education, as opposed to those who had less. In the 1980s, a Congressional study found that a decade-and-a-half of comprehensive, safe sex education resulted in a doubling in the number of sexually active teenage women.

Our society today is filled with teenagers and young adults who know a lot about human sexuality. It is probably fair to say that they know more about sex than any generation that has preceded them, but education is not enough. Sex education can increase the knowledge students have about sexuality, but it does not necessarily affect their values or behavior. Since 1970 the federal government has spent nearly $3 billion on Title X sex education programs. During that period of time nonmarital teen births increased 61 percent and nonmarital pregnancy rates (fifteen-to-nineteen-year-olds) increased 87 percent.

> *When your audience is impressionable teens entering puberty, explicit sex education does more to entice than educate.*

Douglas Kirby wrote these disturbing observations in the *Journal of School Health:*

> "Past studies of sex education suggest several conclusions. They indicate that sex education programs can increase knowledge, but they also indicate that most programs have relatively little impact on values, particularly values regarding one's personal behavior. They also indicate that programs do not affect the incidence of sexual activity. According to one study, sex education programs may increase the use of birth control among some groups, but not among others. Results from another study indicate they have no measurable impact on the use of birth

control. According to one study, they are associated with lower pregnancy rates, while another study indicates they are not. Programs certainly do not appear to have as dramatic an impact on behavior as professionals once had hoped."

So, if sex education is not the solution, what is? Let's look at the benefits of abstinence and the abstinence message in the schools.

Abstinence

Less than a decade ago an abstinence-only program was rare in the public schools. Today, directive abstinence programs can be found in many school districts while battles are fought in other school districts for their inclusion or removal. While proponents of abstinence programs run for school board or influence existing school board members, groups like Planned Parenthood bring lawsuits against districts that use abstinence-based curricula, arguing that they are inaccurate or incomplete.

The emergence of abstinence-only programs as an alternative to comprehensive sex education programs was due to both popularity and politics. Parents concerned about the ineffectiveness of the safe-sex message eagerly embraced the message of abstinence. And political funding helped spread the message and legitimize its educational value.

Parents and children have embraced the abstinence message in significant numbers. One national poll by the University of Chicago found that 68 percent of adults surveyed said premarital sex among teenagers is "always wrong." A poll for *USA Weekend* found that 72 percent of the teens and 78 percent of the adults said they agree with the pro-abstinence message.

Their enthusiasm for abstinence-only education is well founded. Even though the abstinence message has been criticized by some as naive or inadequate, there are good reasons to promote abstinence in schools and society.

First, teenagers want to learn about abstinence. Contrary to the often repeated teenage claim, not "everyone's doing it." A study by the Centers for Disease Control found that 43 percent of teenagers from ages fourteen to seventeen had engaged in sexual intercourse at least once. Put another way, the latest surveys suggest that a majority of teenagers are *not* doing it.

Second, abstinence prevents pregnancy. Proponents of

abstinence-only programs argue that abstinence will significantly lower the teenage pregnancy rate, and they cited numerous anecdotes and statistics to make their case.

Third, abstinence prevents sexually transmitted diseases. After more than three decades the sexual revolution has taken lots of prisoners. Before 1960, doctors were concerned about only two STDs: syphilis and gonorrhea, Today there are more than twenty significant STDs ranging from the relatively harmless to the fatal.

Fourth, abstinence prevents emotional scars. Abstinence speakers relate dozens and dozens of stories of young people who wish they had postponed sex until marriage. Sex is the most intimate form of bonding known to the human race, and it is a special gift to be given to one's spouse.

Teenagers want and need to hear the message of abstinence. They want to promote the message of abstinence. Their health, and even their lives, are at stake.

9

The Politics of Sex Education Debates

Janice M. Irvine

Janice M. Irvine is an associate professor of sociology at the University of Massachusetts, Amherst. She is also the author of Talk About Sex, *from which this viewpoint is excerpted.*

Debates over sex education can rouse fierce displays of emotion. School board meetings on the subject can quickly go from boring to brawl inducing. Community meetings have resembled boxing matches, with neighbor pitted against neighbor. Indeed, debates over sex education have often ended with physical violence. The purposeful distortions of information and deliberate scare tactics that create these scenes are used to frighten parents into believing that any sex education can be harmful to their children. For example, graphic, illicit material has been used out of context and presented to parents as part of the sex education curriculum to encourage them to speak out against such education for their children.

O n the chilly May night in 1993 when the Newton, Massachusetts, school board planned to vote on a highly contested sex education program, anti–sex education activist Brian Camenker was number sixty-three on the list of citizens who had signed up to speak. After three hours of tense debate in an auditorium marked by a heavy police presence, Camenker, who had been instrumental in leading the fight against the program, got his turn. He stepped to the microphone, paused, collapsed to the floor, and was carried out. It was later announced that he had suffered an intense anxiety attack. Camenker's statement, which was read to the school board by someone else, announced, "My feelings on this issue are well-known. So is my disgust for the tactics being used to silence us. We won't stand for it in Newton, we won't stand for it in Massachusetts, and we won't stand for it in America." Camenker's rhetoric reflected the embattled tone of the debates in Newton, which one father had described as a "civil war." And yet his inability to speak his own refusal to be silenced was a poignant expression of the incapacitating emotions sex education controversies can produce.

Conservative Pat Buchanan had said in 1992 that the culture wars were a battle for the soul of America. They were also a battle for America's feelings. Local debates over sex education are often impassioned occasions. The Moral Majority's Jerry Falwell had urged conservative Christians to get mad and to speak harsh language in furthering their moral beliefs. In sex education debates, language and emotions could indeed be ugly. Community meetings have erupted in shouting matches and even physical violence. Neighbors scream at each other during meetings, overwrought residents faint, people shove and hit each other. School board members and prominent activists have received death threats, donned bulletproof vests, and after volatile meetings received police escorts to their cars. Residents often describe the degree of sudden acrimony and resentment in their communities as civic brawls or civil war. School board meetings go from sleepy affairs to late-night shouting matches. (One national network documentary on local sex education conflicts shows a grumpy school board member peering at her watch and announcing to the meeting that it was quarter to one in the morning.) After a particularly bitter public forum in one town, a sex education supporter said, "I now know what it felt like to be in Nazi Germany. I now know how it felt to be a black in Alabama [where racial strife was rampant]." Both sides of the sex education debate have decried the so-called McCarthyist tactics[1] on the parts of their opponents. Not simply hyperbole, these responses signaled the extent to which people came to feel under siege. Much is at stake and, for some, the heated emotions were welcome. One sex education opponent said about her allies, "I was glad they were strident. We really feel our children are under threat." Sex

1. tactics involving personal attacks on individuals by means of widely publicized indiscriminate allegations

education conflicts involve not merely which curriculum a public school adopts; rather, they are highly emotional public arguments about sexuality and young people.

> *Neighbors scream at each other during meetings, overwrought residents faint, people shove and hit each other.*

The discursive politics of sex education are contests over the meanings and emotional culture of sexuality. Such explosive local battles are not spontaneous outbursts of support or resistance. Rooted in history and politics, they are occasions in which activists evoke in audiences intense feelings and encourage their public expression. Discursive politics frame issues and construct a collective mood which shapes the nature and outcome of national and local debates. Intense emotions can attract supporters to a social movement and galvanize them to action. In local sex education conflicts, emotional outbursts can influence whether a curriculum is adopted or voted down. Nationally, politicized emotions have helped stall the progress of comprehensive sex education. In this regard, then, feelings serve as a potential resource for social movements. However, political appeals to emotion are unpredictable and, like Brian Camenker, can collapse unexpectedly. . . .

Sex education evokes strong feelings

Sex education debates are not inherently incendiary; they are flare-ups which have been ignited. This happens through a mix of factors. No one comes to sex education debates devoid of prior experiences which might shape an emotional response. Nor, conversely, is the particular reaction of anyone involved in a community dialogue fixed or determined. Individual predispositions interact with contextual dynamics in a person's response to the emotional triggers which abound in local sex education debates. Predispositions might include factors such as strong political inclinations, personal experiences with sexual diversity, and the level of openness toward sexual pluralism. . . . Religious commitments can mediate emotional responses in important ways. National evangelical and fundamentalist leaders such as Jerry Falwell have encouraged public demonstrations of anger and outrage among their followers. Values, then, can predispose an individual toward specific feelings, while the display of intense emotions can also be a means by which one demonstrates religious or political affiliation. Still, many people come to community debates without extreme predispositions. How is it, then, that these discussions become hostile, even violent events? I suggest that the polarization of debates stems from practices purposely intended to evoke passionate feelings.

> *Sex education debates are not inherently incendiary; they are flare-ups which have been ignited.*

When social movements "evoke" feelings, they do not tap into essences which are outside of discourse. Rather, they engage in strategic practices that will motivate individuals toward . . . "emotion work"—the effort to produce "a desired feeling which is initially absent." Emotion as political practice involves history, culture, and power. Social movements rely on two dimensions of emotional culture—background conventions and immediate dynamics—to foster emotion work and volatile community outbursts. Background conventions are . . . "feeling rules"—the historically specific guidelines and expectations for how individuals will produce and manage affect. In sex education debates, background conventions involve both ideologies about childhood sexuality and standards for public emotional styles. Immediate dynamics include contextual factors such as heated rhetoric. Background conventions and immediate dynamics interact. Provocative language provokes, for example, through what philosopher Judith Butler calls "the citational character of speech." Language invokes and reinforces prior cognitive and affective conventions. Both background and immediate factors operate as cues to individuals and groups for the production of emotionally normative reactions. The taken-for-grantedness of feelings is crucial to the politicization of emotion.

Traditional affective conventions of sexuality are essential background features of impassioned community debates. Conservative opponents depend on a normative emotional climate of sexual shame. Strategic rhetoric draws on prior affective conventions in which sex is taboo and dangerous. Sexuality education, therefore, can be rendered suspicious with little difficulty, and educators themselves can be easily stigmatized by their association with sex. The emotions of sex education debates are intensified by long-standing conventions about children and sexuality. Sex education opponents hope to produce anger, fear, and disgust among parents by tapping those affective expectations inherent in our broad cultural narrative about the violation of childhood innocence. They may also tap, intentionally or not, what cultural theorist James Kincaid calls our "hard-core righteous prurience" about sexuality and children. It is a powerful mix. This diffuse matrix of affective conventions regarding both sexuality and childhood—anger, titillation, fear, shame, disgust—constitutes an enormous strategic advantage for conservatives. The language and images, public arguments and allegations which sex education opponents employ are all designed to invoke this negative affective culture. When the opponents succeed, not only do they potentially win local battles, but they also reinscribe sexual stigma in the broader emotional climate. . . .

Factors that shape the debate

Shaped by background conventions of affect, the quality and expression of emotions in culture wars are also influenced by local cues. The fluidity of emotions and their responsiveness to social expectation render them keenly sensitive to context. In this sense, feelings can be seemingly "contagious" in mass settings. However, the individual and collective emotions of local culture wars are best viewed as contingent rather than as authentic. Next I examine several factors that shape the emotions of sex education debates: provocative speech and speakers, the physical setting, material deterrents such as police presence, the repetition of sexual speech, and media coverage. Background and immediate dynamics work interactively in local debates.

We have already examined . . . instances in which the evocative vocabularies of Christian Right sex education discourses foster particular emotional expectations. Speech about sexuality is used in a way to scare parents with threats to their children and to mobilize these parents, through emotional overt displays, to oppose comprehensive sex education. Language and images are strategically intended to frighten, outrage, and disgust. It should not be surprising that scary rhetoric often does scare and hateful images do evoke hatred. For example, one community activist told me,

> What the Religious Right did was, they started to call up all the churches and they distributed a document that included pornographic information, graphic information that they said was in the curriculum. Of course we knew it wasn't in there. But people were going to this meeting with misinformation, and very angry. I mean, I would have been very angry seeing graphic pornographic literature in what was supposed to be a curriculum. And so then that discussion started from that point. It's very hard to discuss something when people are hysterical and angry about something that they didn't have any information about from the beginning and then here is something they got. That was a fierce fight. . . .

Locations for sex education debates

The physical setting shapes the nature and expression of emotions in sex education debates. In particular, public meetings can be occasions for unrestrained emotional displays. This is not mindless, irrational collectivity. Emotions, rather, are interactive and the conventions of different settings produce different affective responses. Large numbers of people can exacerbate a collective mentality in which what seems called for are demonstrations of fury rather than an exchange of viewpoints. One school board president in Brooklyn said, "In the early meetings people were yelling 'Faggots out!' and stuff like that. We stopped that and tried to create a tone that didn't let any of that happen. But every once in a while people just went off the rails, and publicly—a thousand people in the audience." He continued, "The thing I did understand is that you needed a mass to do that. The same people who were passionately and wildly furious in large group settings were different in smaller group settings. So it needed contagion and it needed support and it needed emotional resonance from large groups, and that was the way in which maybe it was a mistake to do the big hearings because they didnt succeed in moving the debate to another level. Where it succeeded, I think, was in polarizing large factions across the district." A school board member in another town concurred that people could react very differently in mass settings than in individual conversations. She said, "People that I trusted and had good relationships with would at least engage me in dialogue and they never came out and verbally abused me except at public meetings where everybody was yelling and you couldn't figure out what they were calling you." Media and word-of-mouth reports prompt some towns that have not even had such conflicts to take preventive measures such as assembling a police presence. At one town meeting, written warnings circled the auditorium like Burma Shave signs: "ALLOW SPEAKERS TO FINISH THEIR PRESENTATIONS; THIS MEETING IS NOT A DEBATE!; RAISE YOUR HAND AND STAY IN YOUR SEAT." Yet the very presence of these material deterrents sets an emotional tone. Telling people what is prohibited instructs them in what is possible.

> *Conservative opponents depend on a normative emotional climate of sexual shame.*

As part of the politicization of emotions, speakers at public meetings can use fiery rhetoric to inspire gestures of allegiance. Such rhetoric may appeal to feelings of anger, fear, love, or all of these. For example, after recounting numerous depravity narratives criticizing sex educators, national right-wing activist Judith Riesman yelled to a crowd at a Newton public meeting that all those in the audience who would be willing to die for their children should leap to their feet. Nearly the entire audience immediately arose. Most were clapping, some were hissing and grumbling. Riesman was working to establish a set of collective meanings about how loving parents act concerning sex education. She urged the audience to put these feelings of love and concern on tangible display to others, making it difficult for any parents to remain seated. Riesman did make an impact, as the spectacle of a crowd in action, leaping to its collective feet, acted as a further emotional accelerant.

Politicized emotional appeals such as this one are part of how local culture wars can both mobilize and polarize those who might previously have been uninformed or ambivalent. In Newton, for example, one Jewish, pro-choice mother seemed an unlikely recruit to the sex education opposition. But she had basic concerns about the new curriculum. She was afraid the teachers would be untrained or biased. Although she described herself as tolerant of homosexuality, she did not want it taught in the schools. She thought children should learn that the nuclear heterosexual family was the foundation of society. Abortion posed a more difficult problem for her, since, unlike many anti-sex education activists, she was pro-choice. Perhaps the issue could be taught as a debate, she mused. In short, she described herself as having a complicated range of opinions not driven by unyielding ideological or religious convictions. She went to the community forum after seeing a flyer at the local school; she recalled, "I went by myself. I didn't know any of the people. I just sort of showed up. I had no agenda with me whatsoever." A concerned and somewhat confused parent, this woman was galvanized by Riesman: "She looked like my mother, just like my mother. And I see this woman up there, and let's face it, that woman was not ignorant. And she gets up and in the middle of this just flips out. I mean, the woman, I don't think she went crazy but she was slamming her fists down and—do you remember how she was? She was 'Stand up if you would die for your children!' Wow, this is heavy. You know, I just thought, do we want to teach this or don't we?" This mother joined the opposition right after the forum. Demonstrating how quickly locals can assume leadership positions, she soon emerged as the group's spokesperson. Although it is not foolproof, the evocation of strong emotions such as sexual anxieties and protectiveness among parents can be a trigger for Christian Right mobilization.

> **"***Large numbers of people can exacerbate a collective mentality in which what seems called for are demonstrations of fury rather than an exchange of viewpoints.***"**

The media also play an important role in establishing meanings and expectations for local sex education debates. In general, drama and emotions drive the social production of news. "Joy, sorrow, shock, fear, these are the stuff of news," said a former network president. The passions of culture wars, particularly because they are negative and sensational, enhance news value. Headlines and articles emphasize explosions of feelings, particularly rage and hatred, often framed in the language of battle ("A Fight Rages . . . ," "Battlelines Drawn . . . ," "Amid the Uproar . . ."). Not only do they sell newspapers, but they also coach citizens in the emotional possibilities of town meetings ("Parents: Emotion Is Running High," "Parents Clash . . . ," "Outcry Grows . . ."). They can even instruct when emotional expectations fail, as in one headline that noted, "Quiet Sex Ed Hearings Disappoint Those Looking for Fiery Condemnation."

> *// Activists on both sides of the sex education debates view the media as a powerful forum for capturing public support. //*

Activists on both sides of the sex education debates view the media as a powerful forum for capturing public support. They are also alert to media bias and suspicious of their opponents for allegedly manipulating media coverage. During the course of my interviewing, both sides complained that their opponents had staged explosive events to win public sympathy. After a conservative school board chair had abruptly adjourned a volatile meeting, for example, one of his critics charged, "He's very good at spinning the press. And so in the news media that night and in the papers the following day, it looked as if the meeting had been so out of control, with protesters, sixties style, in-your-face protesters of aging flower children, as he put it, that he and the two women needed a police escort to guarantee their safety out of the meeting. Their safety had never been in question." Media coverage of politics, as sociologist Gamson notes, can prompt people to feel angry at someone, even if such anger is displaced. Neither side of the sex education debates wants to be the target.

Activists, therefore, are exquisitely attuned to distortions. In one case, the *New York Times* spotlighted the antagonisms of two antipathetic members of the city's AIDS advisory council in an article headlined "AIDS Curriculum: Fighting Words" and subtitled "Shapers of Teachers' Guidelines Are Hostile and Exhausted." Militaristic metaphors dominated the article, which described the meetings as "trench warfare" and "a theater of anger in a culture war over sex and the public schools," while it described the council members as "opposing field commanders" who are "emotionally exhausted, but nursing hostilities. And both are girding for new battles." It went on to describe how a debate over one section of the curriculum had become so polarized that it "devolved into a shouting match over where to place the asterisk." The two advisory council members were pictured with captions in which one woman said of the other, "Louise is a killer. She's a very vicious person." This woman claims to have really said that her colleague was a killer in terms of how hard she worked, but that the journalist decontextualized the quotation to enhance the bitterness of the disagreements. Even without purposeful distortions, however, these types of articles spread the message that community meetings are polarized by irreconcilable hostilities. . . .

Likewise, sex education critics pursued tactics of repeating the unmentionable. National leaders . . . often excerpted (or invented) passages from curricular materials they found offensive, reproduced them in flyers or mass mailings, and distributed them throughout the country. Sex education opponents read explicit sexual materials aloud at public venues. . . . Late sixties critics organized reading relays so as to circumvent time limits at school board meetings. In the nineties, one community school board chair told me she had to warn a sex education opponent four times that he could not read explicit sections of a book at school board meetings, so he called various media and read them over the phone. Finally, at a public meeting he read a section on sexual foreplay and oral sex. The repetition of sexually charged language and screenings of taboo images in such an anomalous public setting—for example, a school board meeting—might no doubt produce shock. It might also, as Carole Vance suggested . . . create an atmosphere of "excited repression," further complicating the collective mood. In any case, this strategy was one by which conservative sex education opponents, while ostensibly trying to silence talk about sex, also contributed to the diffusion of detailed sexual speech.

How has the controversy evolved?

The emotional texture of any particular local sex education conflict emerges from a complex mix of long-term dynamics and immediate triggers. One example of this involves structural inequalities in communities. In such cases, evocative rhetoric exacerbates already existing local fragmentation and breakdowns in civic debate. Sociologist Robert Putnam notes that "neighborliness," the proportion of Americans who socialize with their neighbors more than once a year, has shown a steady decline over the past twenty years, while the proportion of citizens reporting that most people can be trusted (37 percent in 1993 compared with 58 percent in 1960) has fallen by more than a third. Moreover, inequalities in income and education lead to disparities in civic participation, fueling frustration among those who have less of a voice in American politics. Together, the fraying of community engagement and trust, persistent social and economic inequalities, and inflammatory rhetoric in local sex education conflicts may allow for the expression of grievances not simply about sexuality but about other factors as well. Conflicts involving race and sexuality can manifest this tendency.

Racial dynamics in sex education debates have shifted since the sixties. Then, for an emerging Christian Right infused with the racial politics of the Old Right, sex education provided an opportunity to exploit whites' sexual fears of blacks. Even by the late sixties, however, the widespread acceptability of such explicit appeals was waning. Sociologist Amy Ansell argues that the "new racism" of the Right, now waged in four arenas of the culture wars—immigration, affirmative action, welfare, and traditional values—allows the movement to fight seemingly race-neutral battles while at the same time attempting to dismantle programs in the name of racial justice. By appropriating a language of equal opportunity and individual rights, these battles embody a less explicit racism than that of the Old Right. Sex education offers a unique platform for the staging of contemporary Christian Right racial politics. Because the movement is predominantly white and middle class, it typically targets schools in its own communities for sex education battles, while ignoring communities of color in curricula and outreach.

10

Teen Sexual Risk Taking Is Reduced by Attending School

Douglas Kirby

Douglas Kirby is a senior research scientist at ETR Associates in Scotts Valley, California. He has directed statewide and nationwide studies on adolescents and sexual activity for nearly twenty-five years. Kirby has also authored or co-authored over one hundred volumes, articles, and chapters on adolescent sexual behavior and programs designed to change that behavior.

There is a multitude of evidence suggesting that school attendance reduces teen sexual risk-taking behavior. In developing countries around the world, as the percentage of girls completing elementary school has increased, teen birth rates have dropped. Due to the structure interaction with adults provided by schools, as well as the increase in students' self-esteem that can come from staying in school, sexual risk taking has been reduced in youth who continue their education past elementary school. Sex education programs that stress condom use can also reduce sexual risk taking.

S chools are the one institution in our society regularly attended by most young people—nearly 95% of all youth aged 5 to 17 years are enrolled in elementary or secondary schools (National Center for Education Statistics, 1993). Furthermore, virtually all youth attend schools for years before they initiate sexual risk-taking behaviors, and a majority are

Douglas Kirby, "The Impact of Schools and School Programs upon Adolescent Sexual Behavior," *Journal of Sex Research*, February 2002, pp. 27–33. Copyright © 2002 by the Society for the Scientific Study of Sexuality. Reproduced by permission.

enrolled at the time they initiate intercourse. These facts raise a variety of questions: . . . (a) Does simply being in school have an impact upon adolescent sexual risk-taking? Does greater attachment to school? (b) Does enrollment in schools with particular characteristics reduce the chances of sexual risk-taking? (c) Through what mechanisms do schools reduce sexual risk-taking? (d) Are there school-based programs that do not focus on any aspect of sexuality but that nevertheless reduce sexual risk-taking? (e) Are there school-based programs that do focus upon some aspect of sexuality and do reduce sexual risk-taking? (f) If so, is there broad public support for these programs and how broadly are they implemented?

Impact of school involvement

There are a variety of kinds of evidence suggesting that being in school does reduce sexual risk-taking behavior. In a multitude of developing countries around the world, as the percentage of girls completing elementary school has increased over time the teen birth rates have decreased. In the United States, youth who have dropped out of school are more likely to initiate sex earlier, to fail to use contraception, to become pregnant, and to give birth. Clearly, there are self-selection effects in these analyses, but the evidence also suggests that there is some causal impact. That is, youth who drop out of school are different in many ways from youth who do not drop out of school, even before they drop out, but dropping out appears to increase their sexual risk-taking behavior.

In addition, among youth who are in school, greater attachment is associated with less sexual risk-taking. In particular, investment in school, school involvement, attachment to school, or school performance have been found to be related to age of initiation of sex, frequency of sex, pregnancy, and childbearing. Finally, plans to attend college are also related to initiation of sex, use of condoms, use of contraception, pregnancy, and childbearing.

Characteristics of schools with high pregnancy rates

Just as youth in communities with high rates of poverty and social disorganization are more likely to become pregnant, so youth in schools with high rates of poverty and social disorganization are also more likely to become pregnant. In particular, when female teens attend schools with higher percentages of students receiving a free lunch, with higher school dropout rates, and with higher rates of school vandalism, they are more likely to become pregnant. Reflecting the relative lack of opportunity and greater disorganization in some minority communities in this country, teens in schools with higher percentages of minority students are also more likely to have higher pregnancy rates than teens in schools with lower percentages of minority students. In these studies, it is often difficult to distinguish the impact of school characteristics from the impact of the community characteristics in which they reside.

Aside from the studies which (a) measure the relationship between student characteristics and student sexual behavior or (b) measure the impact of particular programs in schools (e.g., sex- and HIV-education programs, school-based clinics, or school condom-availability programs), remarkably few studies have measured the impact of school structure and school characteristics upon adolescent sexual behavior. Because school characteristics and programs can undoubtedly have an impact upon adolescents' plans for their future and their motivation to avoid childbearing, this is an understudied area of research. More research is clearly needed in this area.

How schools reduce sexual activity among teens

Social scientists and educators have proffered a wide variety of explanations for how schools reduce sexual risk-taking behavior. Some of their explanations have empirical research supporting them, while others are plausible, but lack supporting research. For example, educators concerned with adolescent sexual behavior have suggested that:

1. Schools structure students' time and limit the amount of time that students can be alone and engage in sex.
2. Schools increase interaction with and attachment to adults who discourage risk-taking behavior of any kind (e.g., substance use, sexual risk-taking, or accident-producing behavior). More generally, they create an environment which discourages risk-taking.
3. Schools affect selection of friends and larger peer groups that are important to them. Because peer norms about sex and contraception significantly influence teens' behavior, this impact of schools may be substantial. How-

ever, just how schools affect selection of friends and peers is not clearly understood.

4. Schools can increase belief in the future and help youth plan for higher education and careers. Such planning may increase the motivation to avoid early childbearing. As noted above, multiple studies demonstrate that educational and career aspirations are related to use of contraception, pregnancy, and childbearing.

5. Schools can increase students' self-esteem, sense of competence, and communication and refusal skills. These skills may help students avoid unprotected sex.

Although all of these explanations (as well as others) are plausible, and some have empirical support, in general, this is also an understudied area of research.

Impact of other programs

If school involvement, attachment to school, school performance, and educational and career aspirations are related to sexual risk-taking, then educational programs that improve any of these protective factors may also reduce sexual risk-taking. Thus, there may be a multitude of educational programs that affect adolescent sexual behavior. Unfortunately, most studies of educational interventions designed to improve academic performance and involvement fail to measure impact upon sexual risk-taking, and thus, the actual impact of these programs upon sexual behavior is largely unknown. This is yet another area for productive research.

However, there is one study that measured the impact upon sexual behavior of a program specifically designed to improve attachment to school. The Seattle Social Development Project was designed to increase bonding to elementary school (and family) through improved instructional techniques (and voluntary programs for parents). The results indicated that it did reduce teen pregnancy among youth followed by the study to age 18.

In addition, there are four studies of service learning programs demonstrating that voluntary service combined with small group preparation and reflection can either delay sex or reduce teen pregnancy rates. Many of these programs are implemented in schools and some have been demonstrated to increase attachment to schools or to reduce school failure, among other things.

In sum, the correlational studies showing the relationship between attachment to school, success in school, and career plans, on the one hand, and sexual risk-taking behavior, on the other hand; the one experimental study of the Seattle Social Development Project; and the studies of service learning programs all suggest that if schools can implement programs that keep youth in schools, make them feel more attached to school, help them succeed, and help them develop plans for higher education and future careers, they may delay their students' onset of sex, increase their contraceptive use, and decrease their pregnancy and childbearing.

How sex education programs help

Using large national samples, numerous studies have examined statistically the relationship between previous participation in a sex or STDs [sexually transmitted diseases]/HIV education program and adolescent sexual and contraceptive behavior. The studies measuring the relationship between receipt of sex education and initiation of sex have produced mixed results: Some indicated such education delayed sex, some indicated no impact, and others indicated it hastened the onset of sex. Studies measuring the impact of sex and STD/HIV education programs upon contraceptive use have more consistently found that they increased contraceptive use.

While these studies attempt to measure the impact of the diversity of sex and STD/HIV education programs actually implemented in this nation's schools, these studies are fraught with methodological problems. For example, these studies have extremely limited data on the quality of any of these programs. In addition, measuring the causal impact is challenging, particularly when sex and STD/HIV education programs are more commonly implemented in higher risk schools. Consequently, much greater weight should be given to the evaluations of individual programs that employed experimental or quasi-experimental designs.

The experimental research measuring the impact of school-based abstinence, sex education, and STD/HIV education programs is reviewed in a separate paper. That review concluded that there are no published evaluations of abstinence-only curricula indicating that these programs delayed sex, but it is premature to draw conclusions about the impact of these programs because (a) abstinence-only programs are a very heterogeneous group of programs, (b) too few rigorous studies have been completed, and (c) there is some evidence that the abstinence pledge can lead to a delay in sex in some conditions and that one community-wide abstinence media campaign may have delayed sex among young teens.

Regarding sex- and HIV-education programs, that review concluded that the overwhelming weight of the evidence indicates that sex- and STD/HIV-education programs that emphasize abstinence, but also cover condoms or contraception, do not increase sexual intercourse by hastening the onset of intercourse, increasing the frequency of intercourse, or increasing the number of sexual partners. In addition, some, but not all, of these programs delay the initiation of sex, reduce its frequency, reduce number of sexual partners, or increase use of condoms or other forms of contraception. These effective programs share common identifiable characteristics.

School-based health centers are clinics located in schools that offer services to students in their respective schools, while school-linked clinics are adolescent clinics located near schools that provide many of the same services, and can be integrated into the schools. Both types of clinics typically provide basic primary health care services; some of them also prescribe or dispense contraceptives. In 1999, there were at least 800 school-based health centers serving students in grades 7 through 12.

> *Investment in school, school involvement, attachment to school, or school performance have been found to be related to age of initiation of sex, frequency of sex, pregnancy, and childbearing.*

When these clinics are well staffed and well run and dispense contraceptives, they have many of the characteristics of ideal reproductive health programs: Their location is convenient to the students, they can reach both females and males, they provide comprehensive health services, they are confidential, their staff is selected and trained to work with adolescents, they can easily conduct follow-up, their services are cost free, and they can integrate education, counseling, and medical services. On the other hand, they may not easily reach older males, the males who are most likely to father children born to adolescent females.

School-based and school-linked clinics do provide contraceptives to substantial percentages of the sexually experienced youth in their respective Schools. For example, in a study of four clinics that provided prescriptions or actually dispensed contraceptives, the proportion of sexually experienced females who obtained contraceptives through the clinic varied from 23% to 40%.

Six studies have examined the impact of these health centers. Five of these studies examined programs in three or more schools. The outcomes they measured and their quasi-experimental designs varied considerably, but in general they were not strong designs. In addition, these studies measured population effects. That is, they measured the effects upon the entire school population and not just upon those students who actually used the clinics for family planning services. Consequently, inferences should be drawn cautiously from these studies.

These studies consistently demonstrated that providing contraceptives in school-based or school-linked clinics did not hasten or increase student sexual activity. Other results were more mixed. Most findings indicated that these clinics did not increase school-wide contraceptive use significantly; to the contrary, the data indicated that there was a large substitution effect. On the other hand, one study found that sexually experienced students in a school with a clinic run by Planned Parenthood were more likely to use contraception than students in a comparison school, and a second study found that students became more likely to use contraception after a school-linked family planning clinic was opened. The results suggest that school-based or school-linked clinics that focus upon sexual and contraceptive behavior and give a clear message about avoiding sex or always using condoms or contraception may be effective.

Condoms and school

Given the threat of AIDS, as well as the threat of other STDs and pregnancy, more than 300 schools without school-based clinics have begun making condoms available through school counselors, nurses, teachers, vending machines, or baskets. These schools are in addition to the 92 schools which make condoms available to students through school-based clinics.

The number of condoms obtained by students from schools varies greatly from program to program; in some schools students obtain very few condoms from the school, while in other schools they obtain large numbers. In general, when schools make condoms available in baskets (a barrier-free method), students obtain many more condoms than when they must obtain condoms from school personnel or from vending machines. Finally, if schools have clinics, students obtain many more condoms than when schools do not have clinics.

> *Schools structure students' time and limit the amount of time that students can be alone and engage in sex.*

There have been only four published studies of school condom-availability programs. All four of these studies found that making condoms available in schools did not significantly increase rates of sexual activity. However, the measured impact upon condom use varied with the study.

Only one of these studies evaluated the impact of making condoms available in multiple schools, collected baseline and follow-up data, had a comparison group, and had large sample sizes. That study found that students did obtain very large numbers of condoms from the schools when condoms were made available without any restrictions in open baskets of condoms in school health centers. However, that study also found that condom use among sexually experienced youth did not increase. Students simply obtained condoms from the schools' health centers instead of from other sources. Focus groups with groups of students found that even before condoms were made available in the schools, condoms were readily available from other sources in the communities, and that the reasons youth gave for not using condoms typically did not include lack of access to condoms. Thus, the condom availability program may not have addressed the real needs of the students.

Of the three other published studies, two found significant increases in condom use and the third found non-significant trends in that direction. However, each of these three studies was limited by one or more of the following methodological problems: lack of baseline data, lack of comparison groups, insufficient sample sizes, or changes in parental consent procedures resulting in serious attrition at follow-up. In addition, two of these studies measured the impact of broader, more comprehensive HIV prevention or health promotion programs, not school condom availability alone.

What conclusions should one reach from these four studies of school condom availability? Logically, there are three possibilities. First, the differences in results could be caused by differences in the research methods. Second, the differences in results could be caused by differences in the communities and in student needs. If youth already have ample access to condoms in their communities, then making condoms available in schools may not increase condom use. In contrast, if communities do not provide condoms in convenient, confidential, and comfortable locations, then making them available in schools may increase student access to condoms and subsequently increase use of condoms. Third, the differences in study results could be due to the addition of other programmatic components (e.g., educational components) in two of the studies. This is consistent with the data showing that some sex programs increase condom use.

In sum, the results from these studies are similar to those of school-based clinics—they confirm that making condoms available on school campuses does not increase sexual activity, but their impact upon use of condoms is mixed. It is unclear why results suggest that school condom availability may have increased condom use in some cities, but not others.

Public support for sex education

For decades there has been and continues to be widespread support for sexuality and HIV education in schools. For example, four national Gallup polls conducted between 1981 and 1998 revealed continual increases from 70% in 1981 to 87% in 1998 in the percent of American adults who believed that public high schools should include sex education in their instructional programs. Similarly, a 1999 Hickman-Brown national opinion poll found that 93% of adults supported sexuality education in schools.

The approval for sexuality and HIV education also is manifested in state policy: 18 states require that sexuality education be taught in schools, while 34 states require that schools offer STD/HIV education.

Thus, the controversies surrounding sexuality and HIV education programs do not focus on whether these programs should be offered in school, but rather on what topics should be taught and emphasized. Some groups believe that only abstinence, or only abstinence until marriage, should be taught, whereas other groups believe that condoms and contraception and other topics related to sexuality should be covered in a medically accurate manner.

Despite the growing strength of the abstinence movement across the country, large majorities of adults favor sex and AIDS education that includes discussions of condoms and contraceptives. For example, a 1998 poll of American adults found that 87% thought birth control should be covered, a 1999 poll found that 90% of adults thought condoms should be covered, and another 1999 poll found that 82% of adults believed all aspects of sex education including birth control and safer sex should be taught.

Despite these majorities, an increasing number of states place restrictions on instruction about condoms and contraceptives, and a substantial proportion of schools limit instruction to abstinence. According to a large national study of school district policies, of the 69% of school districts that have policies on sex education, 35% teach abstinence as the only option outside of marriage, and either prohibit instruction on condoms or contraceptives or focus upon their shortcomings.

Among adults in this country, there has also been considerable support for the provision of condoms or contraceptives through school condom-availability programs and school-based health centers. For example, a 1991 Roper poll indicated that 64% of American adults favored making condoms available in high schools, a 1992 Gallup poll found that 68% of adults approved of condom distribution in public schools, and a 1999 poll found that 53% of adults thought school personnel should make condoms available for sexually active young people.

Prevalence of sex education programs in schools

Given both the need for effective educational programs and public support for such programs, schools have responded. According to a 1999 national survey of school teachers in grades 7 to 12, about 93% of their schools offered sexuality or HIV education. Of those schools teaching any topics in sexuality education, between 85% and 100% included instruction on consequences of teenage parenthood, STD, HIV/AIDS, abstinence, and ways to resist peer pressure to have sex. Between 75% and 85% of the schools provided instruction about puberty, dating, sexual abuse, and birth control methods. Teachers reported that the most important messages they wanted to convey were about abstinence and responsibility.

During the same year, survey results from a second survey of teachers and students in grades 7 to 12 were completed. Their results were similar to the study above. They revealed that at least 75% of the students and similar percentages of the teachers indicated the following topics were covered in their instruction: basics of reproduction, STD and HIV/AIDS, abstinence, dealing with pressures to have sex, and birth control.

> *Because peer norms about sex and contraception significantly influence teens' behavior, this impact of schools may be substantial.*

Despite the fact that most adolescents receive at least a minimum amount of sexuality or HIV education, it is widely believed by professionals in the field that most programs are short, are not comprehensive, fail to cover some important topics, and are less effective than they could be. For example, both surveys of teachers discussed above found that only half to two thirds of the teachers covered how to use condoms or how to get and use birth control.

Furthermore, there is very little information about the extent to which sex- and HIV-education curricula that have been found to be effective are implemented with fidelity in additional schools. However, considerable anecdotal information indicates that even when schools purchase these effective curricula, few implement most of the lessons. Thus, there is a widely held belief that schools have established a foundation for programs, but that effective programs need to be implemented more broadly and with greater fidelity throughout the country.

There are at least three important reasons why effective programs are not implemented more broadly. First, schools devote relatively little time to health education more generally, and to sex and HIV education more specifically. Because the effective programs last for numerous class periods, teachers have difficulty fitting them into their semester curricula. Second, the effective programs include activities that some parents and communities oppose, because they fear they will sanction and encourage sexual activity. Third, many teachers and school districts do not realize that some sex- and HIV-education programs have strong evidence for their success.

What the research tells us

The research on the impact of schools upon adolescent sexual behavior is quite uneven. On the one hand, there is relatively little research on the impact upon sexual behavior of school structure and non-sexuality-focused school programs. On the other hand, there is much more research on school programs that address sexuality, especially sex- and HIV-education programs and, to a lesser extent, school-based clinics and school condom-availability programs. Additional research on the impact of school structure and non-sexuality-focused programs may be very productive.

Despite the limitations of this body of research, there is evidence to support several conclusions. Programs that effectively decrease school dropout and improve attachment to school, school performance, and educational and career aspirations are likely to either delay sex, increase condom or contraceptive use, or decrease pregnancy and childbearing. Service learning programs have especially strong evidence for reducing teen pregnancy. Those sex- and STD/HIV-education programs with identified common characteristics can also delay sex, reduce the frequency of sex, increase condom or contraceptive use, or decrease pregnancy and childbearing. School-based clinics and school condom-availability programs do not increase any measure of sexual behavior, but may or may not increase condom or contraceptive use.

Despite the many controversies, there is broad public support for sex education in public schools, including support for instruction about condoms and contraceptives. Consequently, most schools provide some sex education instruction, but many do not cover important topics and relatively few schools implement with fidelity those programs that have been demonstrated to be effective. Thus, implementing effective programs both with fidelity and more widely may reduce sexual risk-taking behavior among adolescents.

11

The Mass Media Educate Youth About Sex

Jane D. Brown and Sarah N. Keller

Jane D. Brown is a professor at the School of Journalism and Mass Communication at the University of North Carolina, Chapel Hill. Sarah N. Keller is an assistant professor in the department of communication at Emerson College in Boston.

The media play a huge part in educating teens about sex and will likely have an even bigger impact in the future. The media need to present a healthier, more responsible view of sexuality and make appropriate sources of information about sex more accessible. Moreover, children need to be taught how to make sense of the various media representations of sex so that they can find useful information without being exposed to harmful material.

The mass media—television, music, magazines, movies and the Internet—are important sex educators. Yet, the media seldom have been concerned with the outcome of their ubiquitous sexual lessons. Typically, those who own and create communications media have been more concerned with attracting audiences and selling products than they have been in promoting healthy sexuality. Most are driven by profit margins, not social responsibility, and are not in the business of promoting healthy sexuality. If irresponsible sexual behavior attracts audiences, then that is what will be produced.

Could the media be healthier sex educators? Absolutely. Will they do it? That's less clear.

Jane D. Brown and Sarah N. Keller, "Can the Mass Media Be Healthy Sex Educators?" *Family Planning Perspectives*, September/October 2000. Copyright © 2000 by The Alan Guttmacher Institute. Reproduced by permission.

A media-saturated world

Young people in the United States today spend 6–7 hours each day, on average, with some form of media. A majority have a television in their bedroom; all have access to music and movies. Computer and Internet use is diffusing rapidly. By 2010, it is expected that most homes with children in the United States will have access to the Internet. It is not clear, however, when and if the current "digital divide" between lower and higher income families and between those who are less literate or non-English-speaking and those who are literate or English-speaking will disappear.

The media-saturated world in which children live is a world in which sexual behavior is frequent and increasingly explicit. Gone are the "I Love Lucy" days of single beds and polite pecks on cheeks. Youth today can hear and see sexual talk and portrayals in every form of media.

> *Could the media be healthier sex educators? Absolutely. Will they do it? That's less clear.*

Adolescents rank the media with parents and peers as important sources of sexual information. This may be because the media are better at depicting the passion and positive possibilities of sex than its problems and consequences. Despite increasing public concern about the potential health risks of early, unprotected sexual activity, only about one in 11 of the programs on television that include sexual content mention possible risks or responsibilities. Sexually transmitted diseases other than HIV and AIDS are almost never discussed, and unintended pregnancies are rarely shown as the outcomes of unprotected sex. Abortion is a taboo topic, too controversial for commercial television and magazines. Homosexual and transgendered youth rarely find themselves represented in the mainstream media. Although a few youth-targeted programs, such as "Dawson's Creek," have recently included gay characters, what some have called "compulsory heterosexuality" prevails.

The clash between the media's depiction of sexual relations and the real-life experiences of youth contributes to their difficulties in making healthy sexual decisions. Although we still have much to learn about how the media influence young people's sexuality, evidence is accumulating that besides imparting basic information about sex, the ubiquitous and risk-free media portrayals, coupled with inadequate alternative models from other sectors, encourage unhealthy sexual attitudes and behavior.

Transforming the media

Government regulation of media content is unlikely and probably the least desirable remedy, so two strategies for working with the media hold greater promise. A number of groups, including the Henry J. Kaiser Family Foundation, Advocates for Youth and the National Campaign to Prevent Teen Pregnancy, have been working with Hollywood scriptwriters and television and music producers as well as magazine editors to encourage more sexually responsible media content. As a result of these efforts, hit shows like "Felicity" have included sensitive portrayals of homosexual youth, have provided explicit lessons in how to put on a condom and have portrayed teenagers postponing sexual intercourse, apparently with no decline in audience interest. Additionally, magazines such as *Teen People* and *YM* have produced excellent articles on such relevant topics as adolescent pregnancy and contraceptives.

The second strategy available to sex educators is the Internet, which has the advantage over other media of allowing any group to make their information and point of view available relatively inexpensively. Children soon will take for granted that they have access to almost any information and any form of entertainment in one place at any time they want it. At this point, unfortunately, it is easier to find sexually explicit, unhealthy sites than it is to locate those that promote sexually responsible behavior in an equally compelling way.

A number of comprehensive sexuality education websites for young people have been launched. Some of the earliest, such as Columbia University's *www.goaskalice.columbia.edu*, were established to provide college students with easily accessible health information and to offer sexual health information. A number of the current sites that focus on sexual health include sections for users to send in questions that a panel of experts will answer. Most of these also include a "frequently asked questions" (FAQ) section, since teenagers often share similar concerns (e.g., *www.sxetc.org*, the site run by the Network for Family Life Education at the Rutgers University School of Social Work).

Sites typically include other features that might attract teenagers to learn more about specific topics, such as "Sex: What to do?! Did your first time get you into a sticky situation?" and "Four birth control methods not recommended for teens" (Planned Parenthood Federation of America's *www.teen wire.org*). Others, such as the American Social Health Association's *www.iwannaknow.org* site, also include chat rooms in which teenagers can discuss sexual concerns with their peers. The iwannaknow.org site's chat room is monitored by an experienced sexuality educator who can stop inappropriate talk and solicitation or interject accurate information.

> *The clash between the media's depiction of sexual relations and the real-life experiences of youth contributes to their difficulties in making healthy sexual decisions.*

At this point, we know little about who has access to such sites and how they are used, but they have promise. A major hurdle will be making sure that youth are aware of and can find the "good" sites. We also have to be careful that the good is not thrown out with the bad, as concern about protecting children from the risks of websurfing increase. According to a recent national survey of young people (10–17 years old) who regularly use the Internet, one out of five said they had been exposed to unwanted sexual solicitations while online in the past year. One in four reported having inadvertently encountered explicit sexual content. Unfortunately, current screening devices are as likely to block sites containing information about breast self-exams, for example, as they are to block the many sites depicting bare breasts.

It is unlikely that the media, including the Internet, will shift toward a healthier depiction of sexuality anytime soon. Nonetheless, it is important that those concerned continue to push for healthier representations in commercial media and to create alternative portrayals and sources of information whenever possible. In the meantime, the most effective strategy may be to help children learn how to navigate this remarkable ocean of information, ideas and images. In some countries, such as Canada and Australia, media literacy is taught at all grade levels and throughout the curriculum, so children learn early that all media are constructed, convey a particular set of values and, in general, are designed to sell products. The need for media literacy is beginning to gain adherents in the United States as well. For example, a number of states have included media education in their public education standards. Children who know more about how the media work, how images are constructed and the potential effects of media exposure should be less negatively affected by media use and should be more able to find what they are looking for without being ambushed by unwanted, unhealthy sexual material or by predators.

In short, the media are important sex educators today and will continue to be in the future. Therefore, efforts both to encourage the media to present a healthier view of sexuality and to create, promote and make accessible healthier sources of sexual information should continue. Most importantly, children should be armed with the navigational and analytic tools they'll need to be able to create sexually healthy lives—despite what most of the media teach.

12

Sex Education Should Address the Needs of Gay Teens

Carol Lee

Carol Lee is a student at New York University's department of journalism and mass communication.

Traditional sex education programs do not take into account the needs of gay teens. These students need information on how to protect themselves from risks associated with sex just as their heterosexual classmates do. Gay teens also need to feel supported and to know that there is nothing wrong with them. Youth who are struggling with their sexual identities are quicker to engage in risky sexual behavior and are more likely to become pregnant.

By age 11, Elina Kuusisto knew that she had no interest in boys. She also knew that being gay was clearly unpopular. But, she says, her sexuality education stopped there. Open about being a lesbian since ninth grade, Kuusisto, now 18, says she sat through sex education classes that addressed her boy-crazy classmates, but failed to acknowledge her confusion.

"They made me feel like I wasn't a real member of society," she says of the teachers and students at her high school in Almelund, Minn., about 50 miles north of Minneapolis. Despite support at home from her mother, the lack of discussion about homosexuality and harassment from her peers and teachers left her depressed and frequently visiting the school counselor.

Carol Lee, "Gay Teens Ignored by High School Sex Ed Classes," www.womensenews.org, February 10, 2002. Copyright © 2002 by Women's eNews. Reproduced by permission.

"I just felt like the only weird kid out there. I didn't have any idea what I was supposed to act like, how I was supposed to dress, how to protect myself," Kuusisto says.

Despite the nearly 1 million gay teenagers in the United States, and the growing visibility of gays and lesbians in the broader culture, few educators are willing to address homosexuality in the classroom. Advocates assert that including gay issues in sexuality education could help address heightened health risks faced by gays and lesbians due to misinformation and lack of information about safe-sex practices; emotional isolation that contributes to high suicide and dropout rates among gay teens; and widespread harassment of gay and lesbian students by their peers and teachers.

Nearly 70 percent of U.S. school districts mandate some form of sex education, but very few include the health risks and lifestyles of lesbians and gays as part of the curriculum. In fact, spurred by federal funding incentives in the 1996 welfare law, school districts in 48 states have adopted an "abstinence-until-marriage" curriculum specifying that "a mutually faithful monogamous relationship in the context of marriage is the expected standard of human sexuality."

Only 20 states mandate sexuality education in their statewide content standards and 37 mandate HIV and sexually transmitted diseases education, according to the Sexuality Information and Education Council of the United States. But none require that teachers address homosexuality.

"Sexuality education as it stands ignores gay youth, both lesbians and gay men," says Heather Sawyer, a Chicago-based senior staff attorney for the LAMBDA Legal Defense and Education Fund, a national organization that advocates for the civil rights of lesbians and gays. "It renders them invisible, and by doing that you ignore particular health issues."

Gay and lesbian teens at risk

Many students, regardless of their orientation, say they don't receive information that encourages healthy sexual development; yet lack of information appears to particularly sting those who feel they are not part of their peers' fascination with the opposite sex. "H," a 16-year-old lesbian from Vancouver, Wash., who asked that her name not be published and would only be interviewed via Instant Messaging for fear of being "outed" to her parents, says she had a sexuality education class in sixth grade, but her teacher never mentioned homosexuality.

"It would be beneficial to have some coverage on the topic of homosexuality," says H, adding that information about sexually transmitted diseases would have been helpful as well. H, during the interview, said she had never heard of a dental-dam, a barrier used during oral sex to reduce the risk of disease.

> **//**Nearly 70 percent of U.S. school districts mandate some form of sex education, but very few include the health risks and lifestyles of lesbians and gays as part of the curriculum. **//**

"I see no problem with engaging in sexual activities with another girl," H wrote. "Maybe if I knew some of the risks, I would think differently."

Stacy Weibley, a sexuality educator and public policy associate at the education council, argues that lesbian teens face increased health risks, largely because of fear and ignorance. "When young people do get the courage to talk with a practitioner or medical provider, they assume they're straight. They're not asking if a girl is using a dental-dam when having sex with her girlfriend," Weibley says.

Lesbian teens more likely to become pregnant

A 1995 study of Minnesota teens published in the Journal of Adolescent Health found that lesbian and bisexual girls were more likely to become pregnant and more likely to have multiple pregnancies than heterosexual girls.

"Youth that are struggling with their sexuality or sexual orientation are at risk for engaging in sexual behavior because they're trying to work things out," says Sawyer. "Lesbian youth, for example, might fight against that by engaging in sexual behavior with older men."

Ruth Bell, author of *Changing Bodies, Changing Lives: A Book for Teens on Sex and Relationships*, argues that the psychological effect of stigmatizing homosexuality in the classroom is as potentially harmful as not educating teens about HIV/AIDS and other sexually transmitted diseases.

"We need to teach ways for teens to protect themselves, but

also give them a place to get support," she says. "It's more than the sexuality education side; it's the support side of it, having someone to say you're not bad."

Studies document the emotional toll on gay teens. A 1993 report by the Massachusetts Governor's Commission on Gay and Lesbian Youth, for instance, found that 97 percent of students in public high schools in the state regularly hear homophobic remarks from their peers. Not surprisingly, many lesbian, gay and bisexual youth skip classes and eventually drop out of school; LAMBDA reports that 40 percent of homeless youth identify as lesbian or gay.

A 1995 report from the Centers for Disease Control and the Massachusetts Department of Education found that lesbian and gay youth are four times more likely than non-lesbian and gay teens to attempt suicide. And the U.S. Department of Health and Human Services has reported that gays and lesbians account for 30 percent of all teen suicides.

> **❜❜** *Sexuality education as it stands ignores gay youth, both lesbians and gay men.* **❜❜**

"It would lessen that hostility if there was an open discussion about sexual orientation and sexuality," says Sawyer. "It's a valuable message not just for kids who may be having issues of sexual orientation, but for all students."

Parents and teachers fear discussion of homosexuality

Including information about homosexuality remains highly controversial among parents, school administrators and teachers. About 1 in 12 high school health teachers taught their classes that homosexuality is wrong in 1995, according to a survey of 211 U.S. school districts published in the *Journal of School Health*. LAMBDA reports that 77 percent of prospective teachers would not encourage a class discussion on homosexuality and 85 percent oppose integrating gay and lesbian themes into their existing curriculums.

Parents and educators who oppose discussion of homosexuality in schools commonly express fear that exposure influences sexual orientation. Some gay teens agree: Danielle Kruszewski, 18, says she doesn't know if she'd be gay if she didn't attend an accepting school in Levittown, Penn., and hadn't met her first girlfriend. "I don't think people are born with it," she says. "It's like drinking Pepsi or Coke. You're not born to like Coke. You're not born to like Pepsi."

> *Youth that are struggling with their sexuality or sexual orientation are at risk for engaging in sexual behavior because they're trying to work things out.*

Yet even at Kruszewski's school, where numerous students are openly gay, health education teacher Edwin Neumann says the faculty skims the chapter on homosexuality, providing little more than a definition of the term. "Basically, we provide an explanation of what [homosexuality] is," he says. Any further discussion about homosexuality, including safe sex, is "something that individual families make decisions on," Neumann says.

Sex education policies vary widely from state to state and from district to district. Under the doctrine of "local control," each school district devises its own sexuality education curriculum in accordance with any statewide content standards, such as HIV and AIDS education. Local, rather than state or federal control, not only dilutes the possibility of consistent sexuality education curriculums, but also allows direct parental input over what children learn.

Nevertheless, while the U.S. Department of Education does not mandate specific standards to the states, in the 1996 welfare legislation the federal government did provide funding incentives for schools that adopted an abstinence-based education program. By 1999, 35 percent of school districts that have a sexuality education policy had implemented the abstinence program, reported Family Planning Perspectives. . . .

Schools that are different

While the vast majority of schools avoid discussing gay issues, a handful of schools have tried a different approach. In 1984, gay and lesbian activists in New York spearheaded the first and largest U.S. high school specifically for gay, lesbian, bisexual and transgender students. The Hetrick Martin Institute in Manhattan houses the Harvey Milk High School, a public school that follows the New York City Board of Education's curriculum to educate about 100 students grades nine through 12.

Before enrollment, students at Harvey Milk must demonstrate that they are unable to succeed in their previous high school because of violence, harassment or other learning obstacles. The dropout rate is minimal and the school currently has a three-year waiting list.

"It's a high school where sexual orientation is taken off the table," says Carl Strange, a spokesman for the Hetrick Martin Institute. "There's no excuse not to excel."

A similarly accepting atmosphere exists at Friends Central School, a private, K–12 grade Quaker school in Newton Square, Penn. Lindsey Stetson, 18, an only child adopted from Hong Kong, attends classes like "Sexuality and Society" and "Gay and Lesbian Representation in Literature" along with sexuality education classes that discuss all sexualities. She has also had an open dialogue about her sexuality with her parents. Stetson is acutely aware that her experience is not commonplace, so she is anxious about going away to college.

"I live in a school, social setting, family and church of very accepting people," Stetson says. "I feel like I haven't experienced the real world of being gay."

Organizations to Contact

The editors have compiled the following list of organizations concerned with the issues debated in this book. The descriptions are derived from materials provided by the organizations. All have publications or information available for interested readers. The list was compiled on the date of publication of the present volume; names, addresses, phone and fax numbers, and e-mail addresses may change. Be aware that many organizations take several weeks or longer to respond to inquiries, so allow as much time as possible.

Advocates for Youth
2000 M St. NW, Suite 750, Washington, DC 20036
(202) 419-3420 • fax: (202) 419-1448
e-mail: questions@advocatesforyouth.org
Web site: www.advocatesforyouth.org

Advocates for Youth is dedicated to creating programs and advocating for policies that help young people make informed and responsible decisions about their reproductive and sexual health. Advocates provides information, training, and strategic assistance to youth-serving organizations, policy makers, youth activists, and the media in the United States and the developing world. Its publications include *Designing Effective Family Life Education Programs* and *Improving Contraceptive Access for Teens*.

The Alan Guttmacher Institute (AGI)
120 Wall St., 21st Fl., New York, NY 10005
(212) 248-1111 • fax: (212) 248-1951
e-mail: info@guttmacher.org • Web site: www.agi-usa.org

The Alan Guttmacher Institute is a nonprofit organization focused on sexual and reproductive health research, policy analysis, and public education. AGI publishes several periodicals focused on sexual and reproductive health and rights. The institute's mission is to protect the reproductive choices of all women and men in the United States and throughout the world. Reports available at the institute's Web site include *Sexuality Education* and *Sexuality and Abstinence Education Policies in U.S. Public School Districts*.

American Association of Sex Educators, Counselors, and Therapists (AASECT)
PO Box 5488, Richmond, VA 23220
Web site: www.aasect.org

AASECT is a not-for-profit, interdisciplinary professional organization. In addition to sexuality educators, sex counselors, and sex therapists, AASECT members include physicians, nurses, social workers, psychologists, allied health professionals, clergy members, lawyers, sociologists, marriage and family counselors and therapists, and family planning specialists and researchers, as well as students in relevant professional disciplines. These individuals share an interest in promoting understanding of human sexuality and healthy sexual behavior. Publications by its members include *From Diapers to Dating: A Parent's Guide to Raising Sexually Healthy Children* and *How to Talk with Teens About Love, Relationships, and S-E-X: A Guide for Parents.*

The Center for AIDS Prevention Studies (CAPS)
University of California, San Francisco
74 New Montgomery, Suite 600, San Francisco, CA 94105
(415) 597-9100 • fax: (415) 597-9213
e-mail: CAPSWeb@psg.ucsf.edu • Web site: www.caps.ucsf.edu

The Center for AIDS Prevention Studies was established to conduct research to help prevent HIV infection and its consequences. Since 1986, the organization has worked to stimulate collaboration among researchers, public health professionals, and community-based organizations involved in AIDS prevention efforts. It has also worked with scientists in developing countries to conduct AIDS prevention research. Publications available on the center's Web site include *Does Sex Education Work?* and *What Are Adolescents' HIV Prevention Needs?*

Family Health International (FHI)
PO Box 13950, Research Triangle Park, NC 27709
(919) 544-7040 • fax: (919) 544-7261
e-mail: publications@fhi.org • Web site: www.fhi.org

Formed in 1971, FHI is among the largest and most established nonprofit organizations active in international public health with a mission to improve lives worldwide through research, education, and services in family health. The organization manages research and field activities in more than seventy countries to meet the public health needs of some of the world's most vulnerable people. Its work helps countries and communities to prevent the spread of HIV/AIDS and sexually transmitted infections and care for those affected by them. Its publications include *Sex Education Helps Prepare Young Adults,* which is available on their Web site.

The Henry J. Kaiser Family Foundation (KFF)
2400 Sand Hill Rd., Menlo Park, CA 94025
(650) 854-9400 • fax: (650) 854-4800
Web site: www.kff.org

The Henry J. Kaiser Family Foundation is a nonprofit, private operating foundation focusing on the major health care issues facing the nation. The foundation is an independent voice and source of facts and analysis for policy makers, the media, the health care community, and the general public. KFF develops and runs its own research and communications programs, often in partnership with outside organizations. The foundation contracts with a wide range of outside individuals and organizations through its programs. The foundation has a number of publications available for purchase on its Web site, including *Sex Education in the U.S.: Policy and Politics* and *Sex Education in America: A View from Inside the Nation's Classrooms.*

National Organization on Adolescent Pregnancy, Parenting, and Prevention, Inc. (NOAPPP)
509 Second St. NE, Washington, DC 20002
(202) 547-8814 • fax: (202) 547-8815
e-mail: noappp@noappp.org • Web site: www.noappp.org

The National Organization on Adolescent Pregnancy, Parenting, and Prevention is dedicated to providing general leadership, education, training, information, advocacy, resources, and support to individuals and organizations in the field of adolescent pregnancy, parenting and prevention. Its Web site includes links to the publications of many organizations with similar missions.

Planned Parenthood Federation of America
434 W. Thirty-third St., New York, NY 10001
(212) 541-7800 • fax: (212) 245-1845
e-mail: communications@ppfa.org
Web site: www.plannedparenthood.org

Planned Parenthood is an organization that believes individuals must have access to comprehensive sexuality education. The organization believes that this sexuality education should seek to increase understanding of sexuality as a normal aspect of human development, enhance awareness of different types of sexual expression, and help individuals accept responsibility for their sexual decisions. Articles available on the Web site include *Sex Education in Schools* and publications written in Spanish.

The Sex Education Coalition
6101 Wilson Ln., Bethesda, MD 20817
fax: (810) 222-1910
Web site: www.sexedcoalition.org

The Sex Education Coalition is composed of educators, health care professionals, trainers, and legislators dedicated to providing information and supporting informed discussion concerning sexuality education. The coalition has a link on its Web site to order publications about sexuality education.

The Sexuality Information and Education Council of the United States (SIECUS)
130 W. Forty-second St., Suite 350, New York, NY 10036
(212) 819-9770 • fax: (212) 819-9776
e-mail: siecus@siecus.org • Web site: www.siecus.org

SIECUS is a national, nonprofit organization which affirms that sexuality is a natural and healthy part of living. Incorporated in 1964, SIECUS develops, collects, and disseminates information; promotes comprehensive education about sexuality; and advocates the right of individuals to make responsible sexual choices. Its Web site has a number of links to publications that can be downloaded free of charge, including *Developing Guidelines for Comprehensive Sexuality Education* and *Filling the Gaps: Hard-to-Teach Topics in Sexuality Education*.

Bibliography

Books

Michael J. Basso	*The Underground Guide to Teenage Sexuality: An Essential Handbook for Today's Teens and Parents.* Minneapolis, MN: Fairview Press, 2003.
Clint E. Bruess and Jerrold S. Greenberg	*Sexuality Education: Theory and Practice.* Sudbury, MA: Jones and Bartlett, 2004.
David Campos	*Sex, Youth, and Sex Education: A Reference Handbook.* Santa Barbara, CA: ABC-CLIO, 2002.
Michael Gurian and Patricia Henley with Terry Trueman	*Boys and Girls Learn Differently! A Guide for Teachers and Parents.* Hoboken, NJ: Jossey-Bass, 2001.
Jennifer K. Harrison	*Sex Education in Secondary Schools.* Philadelphia, PA: Open University Press, 2000.
James Davison Hunter	*The Death of Character: On the Moral Education of America's Children.* New York: Basic Books, 2001.
Mary Jane Kehily	*Sexuality, Gender, and Schooling: Shifting Agendas in Social Learning.* New York: RoutledgeFalmer, 2002.
Meredith Maran	*Class Dismissed: A Year in the Life of an American High School, a Glimpse into the Heart of a Nation.* New York: St. Martin's Press, 2001.
Lynda Measor, Coralie Tiffin, and Katrina Miller	*Young People's Views on Sex Education: Education, Attitudes, and Behavior.* New York: RoutledgeFalmer, 2000.
Diane Ravitch	*The Language Police: How Pressure Groups Restrict What Students Learn.* New York: Knopf, 2003.
Michael Savage	*The Enemy Within: Saving America from the Liberal Assault on Our Schools, Faith, and Military.* Nashville, TN: WND Books, 2003.
Hugh Sockett and Pamela Lepage	*Educational Controversies: Towards a Discourse of Reconciliation.* New York: RoutledgeFalmer, 2002.
Francisco A. Villarruel	*Community Youth Development: Programs, Policies, and Practices.* Thousand Oaks, CA: Sage, 2003.
Janet Divita Woody	*How Can We Talk About That? Overcoming Personal Hangups So We Can Teach Kids the Right Stuff About Sex and Morality.* San Francisco: Jossey-Bass, 2001.
World Bank	*Education and HIV/AIDS: A Window of Hope.* Washington, DC: World Bank, 2002.

Periodicals

Laina Y. Bay-Cheng — "SexEd.com: Values and Norms in Web-based Sexuality Education," *Journal of Sex Research*, August 2001.

Susan M. Blake et al. — "Effects of a Parent-Child Communications Intervention on Young Adolescents' Risk for Early Onset of Sexual Intercourse," *Family Planning Perspectives*, March/April 2001.

Sarah Cordi — "Fight for Your Right . . . to Sex Ed: What You Don't Know Can Hurt You—and Here's What Five High School Girls Did About It . . . ," *Girl's Life*, October/November 2002.

Jacqueline E. Darroch, David J. Landry, and Susheela Singh — "Changing Emphases in Sexuality Education in U.S. Public Secondary Schools, 1988–1999," *Family Planning Perspectives*, September/October 2000.

Cheryl D. Fields — "Let's Talk About Sex," *Black Issues in Higher Education*, January 2002.

Donna Futterman — "Do Abstinence-Only Sex Education Programs Work?" *Family Practice News*, July 2000.

Jatrice Martel Gaiter — "Let's Talk About Sex and Health," *Essence*, June 2001.

Douglas Kirby — "Effective Approaches to Reducing Adolescent Unprotected Sex, Pregnancy, and Childbearing," *Journal of Sex Research*, February 2002.

Patricia Lefevere — "Sex and Sensibility: A Faith-based View: Sex Educator Tackles Tough Issues with Young Teens," *National Catholic Reporter*, September 2003.

Michael Malkin — "Liberal Hypocrisy on Guns and Sex Ed.," *Insight on the News*, July 2001.

Daniel Mindus — "What to Tell the Children: The Battle over Sex Ed," *National Review*, September 2000.

Kate Houston Mitchoff — "Scarleteen: Sex Education in the Real World," *School Library Journal*, July 2003.

Jennifer W. Out and Kathryn D. Lafreniere — "Baby Think It Over: Using Role-Play to Prevent Teen Pregnancy," *Adolescence*, Fall 2001.

Ann Rudrauff — "Student-Centered Sex Education," *Human Development and Family Life Bulletin*, Winter 1999.

SIECUS Developments — "Abstinence-Only-Until-Marriage Programs: A National Trend Facing Local Resistance," Winter/Spring 2004.

David Steinkraus — "Debatable: Is It Time to Abstain from Abstinence?" *Racine Journal Times*, March 13, 2004.

Steve Sternberg — "Sex Education Stirs Controversy," *USA Today*, July 10, 2002.

Andrew Whynot   "Sex Education Program Encourages Abstinence
and Moira Stewart   Among Teenagers," *American Family Physician*,
                       March 2000.

Nancy E. Williamson   "The Need to Evaluate Youth Programs," *Network*,
                       Fall 2000.

Rebecca Wyatt   "New Buzz of Birds and Bees," *Insight on the News*,
                       January 2000.

Internet Sources

Health and Health   "The State of Sex Education in American Schools,"
Care in Schools   February 2004. www.healthinschools.org.

Rethinking Schools   "Two Approaches to Sexuality Education," Winter
Online   2002–2003. www.rethinkingschools.org.

SIECUS   "Virginity Pledges Do Not Reduce Rates of Sexually
                       Transmitted Diseases," March 9, 2004. www.siecus.
                       org.

Index

Abstinence by Choice, 35
Abstinence Clearinghouse, The, 41
abstinence education
  enthusiasm of teens for, 65–66
  federal legislation involving, 14,
    47, 50–51, 99
  history of, 50–51
  is based on wrong assumptions,
    60
  is limited and negative, 52
  is unrealistic, 45–48
  lawsuit supporting, 14
  parent support for, 41–44, 65
  politicization of, 67–77
  prevents pregnancy and
    emotional problems, 65–66
  research proving ineffectiveness
    of, 47–48
  research supporting, 30, 34–40
  as valuable and needing support,
    40
ACLU (American Civil Liberties
  Union), 13
Adolescent Family Act of 1981,
  50–51
Advocates for Youth, 8, 92
AIDS/HIV. *See* HIV/AIDS
AIDS Prevention for Adolescents in
  School, 18
Anderson, Kerby, 59
Ansell, Amy, 77
Association for Reproductive and
  Family Health (ARFH), 23
Avert, 7

Bell, Ruth, 97–98
birth control. *See* abstinence
  education; condoms; sex
  education
bisexuality. *See* sexual diversity
Brown, Jane D., 90
Buchanan, Pat, 68
Bush, George W., 45–46, 47
Butler, Judith, 70

Camenker, Brian, 67–68, 69
Center for AIDS Prevention
  Studies, 15

Centers for Disease Control and
  Prevention (CDC), 8, 11, 22, 98
*Changing Bodies, Changing Lives: A
  Book for Teens on Sex and
  Relationship* (Bell), 97–98
chlamydia, 31, 61
Christian Right. *See* Religious Right
Clinton, Bill, 14
Coalition for Adolescent Sexual
  Health, 41
Cole, Lori, 12–13
collective mentality, 72–76
community involvement, 23,
  25–26
Concerned Women for America
  (CWA), 42
condoms
  effectiveness statistics for, 31,
    61–62
  FDA regulation of, 61
  reserach studies on, 85–86, 87
  school and, 84–85
  sex education classes and, 11, 24
conservative Christians, 68
Crouse, Janice, 42, 44

Delano, Grace, 23

Eagle Forum, 13
Elia, John P., 49
emotional problems, 31–32, 97–98
evangelical movement, 68, 69–72
extremism, 67–77
Eyre, Linda, 8
Eyre, Richard, 8

Falwell, Jerry, 68, 69
Family Accountability
  Communicating Teen Sexuality
  (FACTS) abstinence program, 38
Family Health International (FHI),
  20, 23–24, 27–28
family planning, 59
  see also abstinence education;
    condoms; Planned Parenthood
Family Planning Perspectives, 99
family responsibility, 6–9
  see also parent

FDA (Food and Drug Administration), 61
Feinberg, Ted, 11
Finger, William R., 20
Franken, Al, 45–46
Friends Central School, 100
Frontiers in Reproductive Health, 24
fundamentalism, 68, 69–72

Gallup polls, 86–87
Gay, Lesbian, Straight Education Network, 56
gay people. *See* sexual diversity
Gay-Straight Alliance, 56
Goff, Sarah, 45
gonorrhea, 31
Guttmacher Institute, 12

Harvey Milk High School, 100
health clinics. *See* school-based health clinics
Healthy Oakland Teens (HOT), 17–18
Henry J. Kaiser Family Foundation, 11, 92
Heritage Foundation, 6, 29
herpes, 31
Hetrick Martin Institute, 100
Hickman-Brown poll, 86–87
Hickman-Brown Research Inc., 14
HIV/AIDS, 8, 16, 31, 62
Hoffman, Jodi, 14
homosexuality. *See* sexual diversity
How to Talk to Your Child About Sex: It's Best to Start Early, but It's Never Too Late (Linda and Richard Eyre), 9
human papillomavirus (HPV), 31, 61

If You Seduce a Straight Person, Can You Make Them Gay? (Elia), 49
infertility, 32
Institute for Research and Evaluation, 63
international guidelines, 23–28, 94
International Planned Parenthood Federation (IPPF), 27
Internet, 93–94
Irvine, Janice M., 67

Joint United Nations Programme on HIV/AIDS (UNAIDS), 24–25
Journal of Marriage and the Family, 7

Journal of School Health, 64–65, 98

Keller, Sarah N., 90
Kincaid, James, 71
Kirby, Douglas, 21–22, 63, 64–65, 78
Kreinin, Tamara, 12

LAMBDA Legal Defense and Education Fund, 96, 97, 98
Learning About Family Life, 60
Lee, Carol, 95
lesbians. *See* sexual diversity
Lies and the Lying Liars Who Tell Them: A Fair and Balanced Look at the Right (Franken), 45–46
life-skills education, 23–24, 25–27
Luster, Tom, 7–8

magazines. *See* media
Magnani, Robert, 26–27
Mahler, Hally, 23–24
Maier, Bill, 42–43
Masland, Molly, 10
Massachusetts Governor's Commission on Gay and Lesbian Youth, 98
mass media. *See* media
media
    education for teens about how to evaluate, 90, 94
    failing of, to show sexual reality, 90–92
    need for, in improving sex education, 92–94
    sex education debate coverage by, 73–76
medical care. *See* mental health; school-based health clinics
Medical Institute for Sexual Health, 61
mental health, 31–32, 54–55, 97–98
morality, 98–99
    see also religion
Moral Majority, 68
movies. *See* media
music. *See* media

National Abortion and Reproductive Rights Action League (NARAL), 33–34, 47
National Association of School Psychiatrists, 11
National Campaign to Prevent

Teen Pregnancy, 47, 92
National Center for Education
    Statistics, 78
National Longitudinal Study of
    Adolescent Health, 37
National Parent Teacher
    Association, 8
Neumann, Edwin, 99
New York Times (newspaper), 75–76
Not Me, Not Now, 35–36

Olsen, Joseph, 63
Operation Keepsake, 36

parent
    opposition, 41–44
    preferences, 14
    responsibility, 6–9
    support, 86–87
peer education programs, 17–18,
    28
pelvic inflammatory disease, 31
Phelps, Scott, 13
Planned Parenthood, 7, 12, 33–34,
    64, 84
polarization, 67–77
politicization, 67–77
Population Council, 23, 24
Postponing Sexual Involvement
    (PSI), 17, 38–39, 60–61
poverty, 79–80
pregnancy. *See* teen pregnancy
Project Reality, 13
Project Taking Charge, 39
psychological problems, 31–32,
    54–55, 97–98
public support, 86–87
Putnam, Robert, 77

racism, 77
rape, 54
Readings in Comprehensive Sexuality
    (Elia), 49
Rector, Robert E., 29
religion, 68, 69–72
Religious Right, 68, 69–72
Reproductive Freedom Project, 13
research methodology, 82–83,
    85–86
Resnick, Michael, 34–35
Riesman, Judith, 73
Roper poll, 87

"safe sex" programs, 30, 33–34
Sawyer, Heather, 96, 97

school attendance, 78–89
school-based health clinics, 62–63,
    83–84
Seattle Social Development Project,
    81–82
Senderowitz, Judith, 21
sex crimes, 54, 96
sex education
    arguments against, 29–40, 45–48
    arguments for, 20–21, 49–58
    causes teen pregnancies, 97
    challenges of, 6
    as compromise balancing
        information and abstinence,
        13–14
    conflicts with abstinence-only
        advocates, 12
    confusion in messages of, 10–11
    criteria for effective programs of,
        15, 16–19, 21–24
    as encouraging teen sexual
        activity and diversity, 12–13,
        63–65, 98–99
    failures of, 16–17, 59–66, 88–89,
        95–100
    government spending and, 64
    as having mixed results, 82–84
    is controlled by individual states
        and school districts, 12
    as not encouraging sexual
        activity, 12, 24–25
    statistics supporting, 9, 14, 86,
        87–89, 96
    Web sites for, 27, 90, 91, 92–94
Sex Respect, 37–38
sexual diversity
    fear of, as preventing adequate
        education, 98–99
    high schools for students with
        alternative sexual orientations
        and, 99–100
    media failure to realistically
        portray, 91
    need for inclusion of, in sex
        education, 49
    sex education and, 55–56
    traditional, 51
sexual harassment, 96
Sexuality Information and
    Education Council of the United
    States (SIECUS), 6, 12, 22–24,
    33–34, 52, 96
sexually transmitted diseases
    (STDs)
    increase in, 59, 66

infertility and, 32
statistics about, 10, 11, 16, 30, 31
see also specific STDs
Small, Stephen, 7–8
social problems, 79–80, 83–84
Social Science Medicine (journal), 61
Strange, Carl, 100
syphilis, 31

Talk About Sex (Irvine), 67
teacher training, 23, 26–27
Teen Aid, 37–38
Teen Aid Family Life Education
  Project, 39–40
teen pregnancy, 16, 59, 60, 62–63
teen suicides, 97–98
television. *See* media
transgendered youth, 91
  see also sexual diversity

Unruh, Leslee, 44

U.S. Department of Education, 99
U.S. Department of Health and
  Human Services, 98

Values and Choices, 38
Vance, Carole, 76
virginity pledge programs, 34–35,
  37

Waszak, Cynthia, 20, 26
Weed, Stan, 63
Weibley, Stacy, 97
Weiss, Catherine, 13
Welfare Reform Act of 1996, 14,
  50–51
Weller, Susan, 61
Whitehead, Barbara Dafoe, 60–61
World Health Organization
  (WHO), 12

Zogby International, 41–44